THE EMERALD EVERTONIAN

THE LIFE AND TIMES OF PETER FARRELL

www.mountvernonpublishing.com

THE
EMERALD EVERTONIAN

THE LIFE AND TIMES OF PETER FARRELL

ROB SAWYER

First published as a hardback by Toffeeopolis in 2025.

First Edition

Toffeeopolis is a collective of Evertonians that operates as an imprint of Mount Vernon Publishing Group.

Mount Vernon Publishing Group Ltd, 71-75 Shelton Street, Covent Garden, London, WC2H 9JQ.

ISBN: 978-1-917064-08-8

Copyright © Rob Sawyer, 2025.

The right of Rob Sawyer to be identified as the author of this work has been asserted by him in accordance with the Copyright, Designs and Patents Act 1988. All rights reserved. No part of this publication may be reproduced, stored in or introduced into a retrieval system, or transmitted, in any form, or by any means (electronic, mechanical, photocopying, recording or otherwise) without the prior written permission of the publisher. Any person who does any unauthorized act in relation to this publication may be left liable to criminal prosecution and civil claims for damages.

A CIP catalogue record for this book is available from the British Library.

Cover design and typeset by Thomas Regan at Milkyone. Creative

Images used are from the family collections of former players and club officials featured in this book. Every effort has been made to contact copyright holders for photographs used. If we have overlooked you in any way, please get in touch so that we can rectify this in future editions.

This book is sold subject to the condition that it shall not, by the way of trade or otherwise, be lent, resold, hired out, or otherwise circulated without the author's prior consent in any form of binding or cover other than that in which it was published and without a similar condition including this condition being imposed on the subsequent purchaser.

There is no room in soccer for selfishness, lack of sportsmanship or for lackadaisical lads not prepared to keep fit.

Peter Farrell, 1949.

CONTENTS

Foreword by Séamus Coleman	IX
Introduction	1
Preface – Staring Down the Barrel of a Gun	3
1 James Farrell of the Liverpool Constabulary	4
2 The Boy from the Borough	8
3 Cabinteely United	12
4 Shamrock Rovers	14
5 Entering the International Stage	21
6 Crossing the Irish Sea	26
7 Toffees Tribulations	33
8 Greens Triumph at the Home of The Blues	43
9 Love Match	50
10 The Irish Toffees	55
11 Up for the Cup, But Down in the Dumps	61
12 The Relegation Hangover	66

13 Redemption	73
14 The Quest to Qualify for the World Cup Finals	79
15 Back in the Big Time	83
16 Changes at Goodison	91
17 Heading Towards the Exit	101
18 The Irish Rover	110
19 From the Wirral to Wales	117
20 Back Home	122
21 Flying the Flag for Merseyside	130
22 The Onset of Illness	133
23 The Long Farewell	140
Postscript	147
Tommy Eglington – The Flying Winger of the 1950s	150
Peter Farrell's Playing Career Statistics	166
Acknowledgements	167
Selected Bibliography	169

FOREWORD

BY
SÉAMUS COLEMAN

Any student of Irish football history knows the name of Peter Farrell.

He was well before my time, of course, but older family members would often mention his name, and particularly when I followed his route from the League of Ireland to the top flight of English football.

Like myself, Peter represented both Everton and Sligo Rovers – as did Dixie Dean, so we are in excellent company! But to even be mentioned in the same breath as people like Peter Farrell, Tommy Eglington and Kevin Sheedy is still so surreal for me. I came over to Everton to try and make a career for myself as a professional footballer – it didn't cross my mind that one day I'd be bracketed with such illustrious Irish internationals.

Peter's is a terrific story. From a village in Dún Laoghaire to Goodison Park, Old Trafford, Highbury and the rest is a wonderful journey, and I am sure that it will appeal to football supporters beyond Everton and Ireland.

Only five outfield players have ever appeared more times for Everton than Peter, and that's clearly a testimony to the consistency he had in his game.

It's a privilege to write the foreword for this book and I congratulate Rob on doing a great man justice.

1
INTRODUCTION

In February 2024, Séamus Coleman's 15 years of unstinting dedication to Everton FC were recognised with the presentation to the right-back of the coveted Dixie Dean Memorial Trophy, which originated in 1980 in memory of the record-breaking centre-forward. The man from Killybegs, who has captained the Merseyside club since 2019, was the unanimous choice of the Everton FC Heritage Society, which curates the award.

Coleman was a fitting recipient for the trophy that is engraved with the phrase: 'For sportsmen in the great tradition'. His time with the Toffees brings to mind that of his countryman, Peter Farrell. The Dubliner was another great clubman and key member of the Irish national team who, like Coleman, had a stint at Sligo Rovers. Neither man won the silverware their inspirational efforts for Everton and Ireland deserved, but they have earned the enduring respect of football supporters on both sides of the Irish Sea.

But why was I moved to write about Peter Farell, a quarter of a century on from his death after a long illness? The words of respected Irish sports journalist Peter Byrne, from 2002, give a flavour of why it is time to revisit the life and times of someone long overdue being given 'Everton Giant' status, to go alongside his induction to the Hall of Fame by the Football Association of Ireland.

Peter Farrell, I believe, was one of the great players of Ireland football – not always recognised as such by modern generations, but certainly in that era – the '40s and '50s. A superb footballer; he was strong, he had pace, but most of all he had skill and vision. At a time when it wasn't particularly fashionable to bring the ball down and play with it, Farrell was a great example. The other thing about him was that he was a great competitor; the bigger the occasion, the better Peter Farrell played. And he was one of nature's gentlemen – an adornment to the game who never, in my memory, ever got into trouble with referees. He was involved in the hardest of games, took the hardest of tackles and tackled hard himself but never lost his cool. A gentleman and a superb footballer.

PREFACE

STARING DOWN THE BARREL OF A GUN
LIVERPOOL, AUTUMN 1891

The thief hurriedly exited the premises he had broken into – only to find himself faced with a moustached officer of the law. Caught red-handed, with his pulse racing, he reached into his right pocket and drew out a loaded revolver. Without hesitation, he took aim and fired, seeking to disable – or even kill – the policeman, in order to make good his escape. The trigger jammed and the weapon failed to deliver its deadly payload. In a flash, the constable stepped forward and wrestled the gun from his assailant's clutches before making the arrest. Thus, the grandfather of Peter Farrell, one of the greatest captains of the Everton and Ireland football teams escaped with his life by the narrowest of margins.

1
JAMES FARRELL OF THE LIVERPOOL CONSTABULARY

James Farrell had come to Liverpool from Ireland around 1880 and embarked on a lengthy and successful career with the local constabulary. Hailing from a farming family in County Carlow (his mother had the unusual maiden name of Soy), he had wed Julia Cruise (born in 1856) in her hometown in Wicklow. Two years after their marriage, the 1881 census has the couple living with their infant son, Patrick, at 29 Havelock Street in the Everton district of the Liverpool. Once a village in its own right, Everton had been swallowed up by the growth of the booming port city. The Farrell's home was a brisk 15-minute walk from where Goodison Park now stands in Walton, and a ten-minute stroll in the opposite direction to the lock-up tower which, since 1938, has graced the crest of Everton FC.

The terraced street was famous in the city for

James Farrell of the Liverpool Constabulary, grandfather of Peter Farrell

its steepness. Such was the incline that those making the ascent from Netherfield Road North towards St Domingo Road and St George's Church were provided with iron grab-rails along the pavement. As with much of the Everton area, Havelock Street fell to clearances and redevelopment in the early 1970s, with the population being dispersed, often beyond the city boundaries. Its former location is now within an area of public parkland with views overlooking the new Everton FC stadium, at Bramley-Moore Dock.

A decade after the 1881 census was taken, the Farrells had welcomed two more sons into the family: Loughlin (born in 1882, taking his Christian name from Julia's father) and John (born in 1889). The couple would have six children in all, but only Patrick, Loughlin and John made it to adulthood. They were, at this point, resident near to Edge Lane at 98 Troughton Street, another road that fell victim to redevelopment in the post-war era.

James and Julia Farrell and three of their children

As referenced in the preface, James, then holding the rank of police constable, achieved a degree of local fame in the autumn of 1891 when he apprehended an armed thief. Several news outlets reported that on the evening of 6 October, John Hayes and James Willcock (spelled Wilcox in some reports), who were employed as carriage cleaners for the London and North Western Railway company (LNWR), plus Charles Taylor, an accomplice, had broken into the premises of Messrs Johnson and Blackburn, provisions merchants, at 109 Wavertree Road. The pair set about stealing tins of salmon and other items. On hearing a noise from within the building, Constable Farrell (PC 88B) approached the rear of the premises, disturbing Hayes as he was exiting. Farrell tried to grab Hayes, who instinctively reached for the 'Bulldog' revolver in his pocket and pulled the trigger from point-blank range. Fortunately for the officer of the law, the gun misfired. Quick as a flash, Farrell manhandled Hayes to the ground and was able to knock the weapon out of the burglar's hand before making the arrest. According to court transcripts, in Hayes' possession were found several tins of salmon, a bunch of skeleton keys, a slingshot, a clasp knife, a jimmy, 12 cartridges and some money. Hayes reportedly told James, 'I see it is of no use. I am caught, and I'll tell the truth. Those things were got in the shop that you saw us leaving. The other two men have got more stuff.'

James used his whistle to raise the alarm, and a fellow officer (referred to in court as PC 236B) gave chase to the two other burglars, eventually detaining them. This constable also found a five-chambered revolver, fully loaded, in a nearby alley, as well as a few more tins of salmon.

All three perpetrators would subsequently have their day in court, with Hayes and Willcock charged with attempted murder in addition to burglary. When questioned, although confessing to the theft, the pair pleaded not guilty to the attempted murder charge. The *Liverpool Mercury* reported that a Detective Bryson had asked Hayes who had arrested him. When Hayes confirmed it was a policeman called Farrell, Bryson enquired as to whether the officer appeared afraid when confronted with a firearm. 'Afraid!' exclaimed Hayes, laughing. 'He gave me such a pounding. I never intended to kill the man, and only intended to frighten him and get away.' Giving evidence, Robert Jones, a Liverpool gunmaker, asserted that the revolver would 'click' and misfire if the trigger was not pulled with considerable force.

The gun used to try to shoot James Farrell in 1891, and the wallet presented to the police constable in recognition of his bravery in tackling the burglars

A close-up of the inscription added to the gun

The case was passed to the Crown Court, to be heard at Liverpool Assizes in early December. Hayes, Taylor, Wilcock, along with two others (Robert Ross and Herbert Hall) stood trial for burglary and/or handling stolen goods in and around Liverpool between August and early October. Hayes faced the additional and more serious charge of attempting to fire at a police officer. Defending Hayes, his representative argued that Farrell had heard the accused make a clicking sound with his mouth rather than the firearm. The jury disagreed: Hayes was found guilty of 'having attempted to discharge a forearm with intent to do grievous bodily harm' – a lesser charge to that initially put forward. Hayes was sentenced to a five-year prison term, Taylor received 12 months behind bars with hard labour, while Hall, Willcock and Ross got three months with hard labour.

As a token of appreciation for his bravery, James Farrell was presented by his employer with the faulty revolver that was aimed at him, with an inscription added in recognition of his valour. Wavertree's tradesmen, meanwhile, presented him with an inscribed wallet as a gesture of thanks for helping to put the band of habitual burglars behind bars. Both the decommissioned revolver and wallet remain safely in possession of the Farrell family.

By 1901, with his reputation burnished by the gun incident, James had been promoted to police sergeant, responsible for the bridewell (Liverpool parlance for a police station with its own set of cells) located on Argyle Street in the city centre. Charles Dickens had spent a night at the station in 1860 while researching for one of his books. The family lived in the upstairs flat, so James had the shortest of commutes to work. By this time, teenager Loughlin was employed as a salesman in a carpet showroom. The bridewell is no longer in police use but now stands as a popular city-centre watering hole. The Bridewell pub has retained many of its original features as well as displaying some football-themed memorabilia. The hostelry was also the founding place of famed 1980s chart-toppers, Frankie Goes to Hollywood.

2
THE BOY FROM THE BOROUGH

On James' retirement, sometime in the first decade of the twentieth century, the Farrell family returned to Ireland. They settled in Dalkey, to the south-east of Dublin. It lies within an area known locally as The Borough (or Boro', for short), which also incorporates the port town of Dún Laoghaire.

James and Julia did not appear to take things too easy in their dotage. For example, in June 1929 (a few months before the Wall Street Crash), the couple – now in their mid-seventies – boarded a liner bound for New York to visit Julia's sister who had emigrated there. Julia lived to 85, passing away in 1941; James died five years later.

Loughlin would marry Theresa Glynn

Loughlin Farrell, father of Peter, who moved from Liverpool to Ireland in the early 1900s

in March 1915 – they went on to have three children, Jim (known as Gus), Sheila and Peter Desmond. Peter, the youngest, was born on 16 August 1922 in Railway Road, Dalkey. Loughlin did his best to foster Peter's love of football, and also endeavoured, through word and deed, to teach him the essentials of good sportsmanship and manners, on and off the field of play. He also took his youngest child to his first soccer match. Following in his father's footsteps, the boy would have a youthful attachment to Bray Unknowns FC. His thrill was heading to Dalkey railway station on a Saturday to see the five Dublin-based players pass through on the train on their way to the match. Then he would head home, satisfied.

Unsurprisingly, the paternal side of Peter's family were loyal Evertonians – notably Peter's uncle, Jack Farrell, who lived on Dundale Road in the Old Swan area of Liverpool. Many of the Merseyside branch of the family would come to stay in Dalkey each summer, so it is no surprise that young Peter's childhood English team was Everton. However, in his words he and his pals were 'paper followers' of the great English sides, as they rarely came to play in Ireland. He read all he could about Johnny Carey of Manchester United and Ireland (known as Jackie Carey in Ireland), Hearts' Tommy Walker, Stoke City's Stanley Matthews and Everton's Dixie Dean. The latter two would be his boyhood idols, and his respect for the legendary winger and centre-forward would never wane. Peter's primary focus as a youngster, however, was on playing football with friends: 'One of my earliest memories is of kicking a small ball around on a piece of waste ground not far from my home. As I grew up, I naturally followed the doings of our local side and, like other small boys, thought there was no other team like them.'

One of the proudest days of Peter's early life came when he was presented with a first pair of football boots by his parents: 'I'm afraid that I wore out my football boots pretty quickly for they were hardly off my feet out of school hours apart from the time when I was swotting for my examination.' He recounted the tale of procuring a football when sharing his life story with the *Liverpool Echo* in 1954:

I would be about 10 years of age when I became the proud possessor of a football of my own. I felt I would like to show a little independence and secure my own ball without the help of my parents.

About that time, a firm of meat extract manufacturers had started a competition for youngsters. If you collected coupons from their products, you could send off for various presents the value of which varied according to the number of coupons. I had obtained a pamphlet from our local grocer explaining the scheme and found that if I collected 120 coupons, I could get a size 3 football. At the rate at which we used this firm's products at home, I reckoned it would take me too long before I could become the proud possessor of a ball of my own, so I canvassed all my relations in Dalkey and even wrote to those in Liverpool, enlisting their aid. A couple of school chums also offered to help and, to cut a long story short, within a very little time, I was posting off the requisite 120 coupons on the form concerned. You can probably imagine the delight with which I tore open the wrapping of the brown paper parcel which arrived a few days later. As soon as I had shown the ball to Mother – Father and the rest of the family had already gone to work when it arrived – I dashed along to the shoemaker around the corner, who kept a football pump on the premises and had it blown up.

Dalkey Rangers, which he captained as a free-scoring inside-right forward, came out top of the local boys' league. Peter was duly presented with his first football souvenir: 'It was a medal costing only 2s 6d but, at that time, it meant as much to me as a Wembley cup winner's medal does to those who are fortunate enough to get one. I have still got it; it will always remain one of my most treasured football mementoes.'

Peter was educated at Harold Boys' National School, followed by Christian Brothers School (CBS) Eblana in Dún Laoghaire. However, the untimely death of his father appeared to signal the end of his scholastic studies at just 13 years of age. At this time, his elder brother Jim (Gus) and sister Sheila were relatively new to working life and were bringing home only modest wages. Expecting school fees to be become prohibitive for his widowed mother, Peter was prepared to step away from school and get a job in order to contribute to the family pot. His mother, however, was determined that, if it was humanly possible, her son would continue with his education. To that end, she pushed him towards studying for a scholarship examination that would ensure – assuming success – he could benefit from four more years of education at CBS. He worked harder than ever and was 33rd of 37 successful students among the 500 candidates. As only nine lads from Eblana CBS had succeeded out of an entry of just over 50, he felt that he had done his bit for the school as well as for himself and his family.

The sporting downside of Eblana CBS was that soccer was most certainly not on the curriculum. Peter played in a school rugby team as a scrum-half for two seasons, though the establishment focused on Gaelic football. Brothers Flynn and Horgan persuaded him to concentrate on this sport for a while as a centre-field player. Another teacher at CBS, Aiden Timmons, ran Gaelic football teams at under-14 and under-16 levels under the name Starlights. He submitted match reports to the East Coast Express newspaper and would often make glowing reference to a certain Peter Farrell, who at 14 was playing in the under-16 side, despite being young enough to play in a younger age bracket. However, Peter's divided sporting loyalties were becoming clear, as evidenced by one of Timmons' reports stating: 'The four boys who did not turn up, among them Peter Farrell, were not injured but had been attracted to another code.' Also handy with the oval ball, he was a capable rugby scrum-half, while he learned to become a strong swimmer and diver from taking to the waters between Dún Laoghaire and Dalkey.

Peter would later confess to his heart being 'out of doors on the football field' rather than on his academic studies. When schoolwork ended at 4.30pm, he hastened to the local football pitch and endeavoured to make up for lost time by practising football at every possible opportunity. That all said, he stuck at his schoolwork, anxious to do well for the sake of his mother, who had set such store on him remaining at school in spite of the death of his father. He would express heartfelt thanks: 'I cannot pay too high a tribute to the wonderful part my widowed mother played in those early formative years. The most solid foundation for success in any walk of life, and particularly in sport, is a contented and happy mind. My dear mother, by her deep love of family life and by her continual kindnesses and sacrifices, made us very happy and put me under a debt of gratitude which I can never fully repay.'

3
CABINTEELY UNITED

One evening, a knock on the front door signalled the approach of Christy Devlin, coach of Cabinteely United. Devlin's persuasive pitch convinced the 13-year-old and his mother that a switch to the team located four miles away was the right step up the football ladder to take. Looking back, Peter was full of praise for the impact of Devlin on his football career: 'I never regretted for one moment throwing my lot in with Mr Devlin and I can't pay too high a tribute to the wonderful work this humble man did for all the boys in this team – he was only an ordinary working man, earning his living as a gravedigger.' Mrs Devlin also drew praise for her self-sacrifice, washing and ironing the kit every week and feeding several of the boys before matches.

The team's 'pavilion' was a huge tree with thickly covered branches, located at the back of one of the goals. Here the lads deposited their clothes, with valuables – which rarely exceeded a shilling or so – entrusted to the club secretary. Playing the association brand of football on Sundays as an inside-forward, Peter also appeared for his school team in the Gaelic code as a defender. This has parallels with Séamus Coleman, who only made the switch from Gaelic football, his first love, to soccer at 18, when offered professional terms by Sligo Rovers. In much the same way that

Coleman has spoken positively of how the Gaelic game developed many of the strengths he shows at Everton and for Ireland, Peter credited this with improving him as a soccer player. In particular, it aided his understanding of defensive responsibilities, which would prove useful when he was converted from a forward to a wing-half a few years later.

As Peter recalled to the *Liverpool Echo*, whereas Cabinteely United made do with getting changed for matches under a tree, his school team playing the Gaelic code enjoyed far more luxury: 'These Gaelic school games also recall very pleasant memories. They were played on much better grounds than our soccer one at Cabinteely. We also had a well-equipped pavilion with showers on our school sports ground at Dun Laoghaire. Furthermore, after every away game we were treated to tea by the powers that be. Although usually consisting of tea, bread and butter and cakes, this simple meal in those days seemed quite a party.'

Towards the end of a successful 1938/39 season, in which Cabinteely United finished as runners-up in the league, they advanced to meet Munster Victoria in the final of the Leinster Schoolboys' Cup. Ten chartered buses made the short trip from Cabinteely to Dublin, where the final was to take place. Although the 300 Cabinteely supporters were outnumbered by 3,000-plus Munster followers, they made themselves heard and inspired the team. This was just as well as Munster were overwhelming favourites, able to run four teams, compared to United's entire roster of just 15 players. The Munster lads were physically bigger, stronger and had access to superior training and coaching facilities but were held to a draw by Cabinteely. Peter, who had been appointed team captain the previous season and popped up with a last-gasp equaliser in the final, recalled: 'It was a great day for me personally as well as for the team. Playing at inside-left, which was then my normal position, I scored a goal in the last minute which enabled us to draw 2–2.'

And so, to the replay – staged at the same venue. Again, 300 loyal Cabinteely supporters went along to cheer Peter and his teammates, and were rewarded by a 1–0 victory, the decisive goal scored by Jim Leary, who could have made a career in football but decided to get a trade.

As the triumphant team travelled back home with the trophy, its coach was flagged down in the hamlet of Kill of the Grange on the edge of Cabinteely and the players were then carried, shoulder-high, into the village centre. Later, the manager took the team home, where Mrs Devlin, despite the late hour, had cooked a wonderful meal for the whole team. Christy Devlin told Peter in his later years that it was the happiest day of his and his wife's lives.

Peter's Cabinteely friends had another reason to be delighted with the victory. Tradition had it that the winning captain would be presented with the much-coveted match ball – so the skipper could be counted on to bring it along to their kickabouts.

That same spring, Cabinteely overcame champions Johnville in the replayed final of the Schoolboys League Cup to bring Peter's time there to a fitting end.

4
SHAMROCK ROVERS

Jimmy Dunne, the former Sheffield United, Arsenal and Ireland international player who was, by then, representing Shamrock Rovers, passed on favourable reports of Peter to his club. A Mr Fitzpatrick called at the Farrell house a few days later following up on the recommendation and an offer was forthcoming for Peter to join the famous South Dublin side. Having joined the League of Ireland in 1922 and won at the first attempt, the club – known for its green and white hooped shirts (previously, vertical stripes) – was on the way to becoming the most successful in Ireland for domestic honours. When Peter duly signed professional forms, on his 17th birthday, he was given a £10 note as a signing-on fee. When he took it home, his mother took some convincing that he hadn't stolen it, as she struggled to accept that her son might be paid for playing football.

The Dalkey teenager found himself training in August 1939 with the stars of the League of Ireland winning side of the previous season. He recalled one particular incident during the first training session, which left a lasting impression:

I had been kicking a ball about for ten minutes or so with my colleagues when Jimmy Dunne (who incidentally was one of my football idols) came across to me and said:

'I believe your name is Peter, mine is Jimmy. Anything I can do to help you will be a pleasure.' A simple enough gesture in itself, but one that touched me very deeply. This friendliness and team spirit is the rock of which Shamrock Rovers has been built and which down the years has made them one of the greatest teams in Ireland on the playing field.

In the 1930s, Rovers had been taken over by the Cunningham family. Joe Cunningham was a wealthy Irish bookmaker and became club chairman. However, it was his wife – and mother to their seven children – May, who was de facto general manager of the club. Operating in a primarily male environment, May Cunningham was no pushover – anecdotal reports suggest she brandished her umbrella after the

A young Peter Farrell with two Shamrock Rovers teammates

final whistle at any opponents she was displeased with. Originally from the Southside district of Dublin, Rovers were playing further out in Milltown. The stadium was officially named Glenmalure Park, a nod to the Cunningham's ancestral home in the Glenmalure Valley in Wicklow, but most people simply referred to it as Milltown.

Having anticipated being fielded in one of the junior sides, Peter was pleasantly surprised to be selected for the reserves. In his debut, a 3–1 win over Drumcondra Reserves, he felt thrilled to be wearing the green and white shirt, but somewhat in awe of the exalted company. Still a schoolboy, he was advised by club director Charles Fitzsimons (a clothing-business owner and father of Maureen O'Hara, the actress who became a huge Hollywood star in the 1940s to 1960s) that Rovers would allow him five shillings (25p) per week to cover travelling expenses to and from matches and training sessions. By taking a roundabout route to the Milltown ground, involving some extra walking, he was able to pocket a surplus of two shillings every week – a welcome boost to the household coffers.

Not yet 17, Peter was easily knocked off the ball by older and often fully grown opponents. Time and experience were required for him to adjust to the speed and physicality of the game in the club's second team. Nonetheless, he did adapt and was picked as reserve for the first team's match against Cobh Ramblers in the second round of the FAI Cup. Before kick-off, in strode Jimmy Dunne, who declared that he had a sore heel and could not play. Peter was promptly advised that he would be filling in at inside-right. 'Jimmy immediately came over to me and, putting his hand on my shoulder, said, "Just go out and play your own game, Peter, and you'll be all right. All the lads will help you. The very best of luck." An easy 8–4 victory followed and, as he exited the pitch, Peter was asked for his first-ever autograph by a young supporter. The following week, Jimmy Dunne was again deemed unfit to play so the stand-in teenager was retained at inside-right for the league fixture away to Cork United. He then returned to continue his development in the reserve side.

Having turned professional at 17, Peter broke into the first team at the beginning of his second season with Rovers. A talented tennis player, he had reached the handicap singles final at Blackrock Tennis Club – the same day as Shamrock Rovers' season-opener against Shelbourne. After winning the football match 3–1, there was time for the briefest of baths before catching the bus to the tennis club and hurriedly changing into his whites:

> It was a long-drawn-out, arduous struggle which lasted almost two hours and, as I hit the last winning shot to ensure victory, I felt a very exhausted but happy lad. I certainly enjoyed my long-delayed meal at the tennis club. It seemed to give me a fresh supply of energy for I stayed on to have a great night at the annual dance and distribution of prizes afterwards which lasted until 2am. I often look back with envy on that day and wonder with the passing of the years how my reserves of stamina would now stand up to such a test.

Peter would never lose his passion for tennis and used it as a way to retain peak fitness during football's close season.

Having finished at school, and now 18, the budding footballer eschewed seeking professional qualifications (which his mother had expected) as it would interfere with sport; instead, after thinking of going into insurance, he became a clerk at Cooney-Jennings, a firm of builders, with the possibility of getting qualifications to become a quantity surveyor in time.

Every Tuesday and Thursday night, a dash home from the office and a hurried meal preceded training with Shamrock Rovers. According to teammate Tommy Eglington, training sessions were basic, to say the least: 'Buller Byrne would stand at one end of the ground and Bob Fullam at the other to make sure that the players did their laps.'

Peter often featured in the side in the 1941/42 campaign, but the following season the youngster had managed to displace Jimmy Buchanan, who had suffered a loss of form, and had become a key player. By now, most of Europe was at war. Eglington also commented that, although Ireland was officially neutral in World War Two, it was impacted by fuel shortages and public transport reductions, which necessitated improvisation for travel to away matches: 'We travelled to Cork by taxis. It was not easy having to get out and play after such a journey, but it was something that was done then.'

In a match at Dalymount Park – home of Dublin rivals Bohemians – in November 1942, Peter had a near-miss after a half-time mishap of his own making.

Peter, in the colours of Shamrock Rovers, heading the ball

At half-time during a league game with Bohemians that season, I went to rinse my mouth from what I thought was a small bottle of water. When the fluid reached my tongue, I discovered it was ammonia, which was well diluted, luckily. There was consternation in the dressing room and a doctor was quickly called for [newspaper reports indicate it was the St John Ambulance who attended]. Fortunately for me only a very small drop had got beyond my palate, though it burned horribly.

After a quarter of an hour of the second half, I resumed and finished the game, but I didn't feel too good after the match and was taken to hospital where I was detained for two nights for observation. I can still recall how some of the patients in the ward looked at me, obviously wondering if I was 'all there' when I told them what had happened.

Peter secured a first international football honour when selected at inside-left for the League of Ireland (Republic of Ireland) representative XI to play against an Irish League (Northern Ireland) XI on 17 March 1943 (St Patrick's Day). It was not a very happy debut, however, as they were beaten 1–0 and Peter was not satisfied with his own performance. Along with five others, he was dropped for the return game in Belfast on Easter Monday.

Towards the end of that domestic season, injury to left-back Shay Healey saw the team reshuffled and Peter was switched to left-half for a league game against St James's Gate (the team from which Johnny Carey was transferred to Manchester United). He recalled: 'This was the first occasion I had ever figured in this position and although it did seem a bit strange at first, particularly having to defend when so accustomed to attacking, I gradually settled down, and towards the end of the match was really enjoying myself.'

He made the new position his own and would revel in it for the majority of his playing career. He played behind Davy Cochrane, Paddy Coad, Jimmy Dunne, Jimmy McAlinden and Tommy Eglington. 'I was 16 years in English football,' said Peter, 'but I never played behind a better forward line than that. If you couldn't play behind that lot, you couldn't play at all.' The left-sided partnership with quicksilver winger Eglington, who would become a close friend, would continue to the end of the 1950s, at three clubs. Apart from a weekly wage of £4 and bonuses from Shamrock Rovers, Peter was, by now, earning a similar amount from his office job, and was in a position to repay his mother for all she had done for him.

The Hoops never secured a league title in Peter's time there, finishing runners-up in 1941/42 and coming third in 1943/44 and 1944/45. They did enjoy better fortune in the FAI Cup, however. In 1943/44 season Rovers reached the final, with near rivals and league champions, Shelbourne, the opponents. On the Thursday before the big game, Peter was forced to take to his bed with a severe sore throat, which showed little sign of improving on the Friday. He feared he would miss the final but received a visit on the Saturday from the club doctor and Mrs Cunningham. He was overjoyed when the doctor informed him that he had an even-money chance of playing on Sunday, as the swelling of his glands had abated.

Come the next morning, he awoke feeling, in his words, 'grand' – but he fretted about how he would fare with a strenuous 90 minutes of cup final football. Walking along O'Connell Street to meet up with his clubmates in their Dublin hotel, he saw a large procession of Rovers supporters headed by a band, making its way towards

Dalymount Park, the venue of the big game. After a thorough examination from the doctor, Peter was deemed fit to take up his usual position at left-half on that beautiful April Sunday.

The doctor's prognosis proved sound as the wing-half, who was now frequently captaining the side, felt no ill effects from his recent illness. Rovers led Shelbourne 3–1 at half-time, and looked well set for an easy victory, but ended up clinging on 3–2 after a more tentative second half display. Joined once again by the band, the players and trophy were perched on hackney cabs as they made their way in triumph from Dalymount Park through the main streets of Dublin to Milltown, accompanied by a large crowd of enthusiastic supporters. A victory dance went on into the small hours of Monday, with little chance for sleep before Peter reported for work: 'I can assure you that as I sat at my office desk that same day my mind was far from my work as I re-lived every minute of that momentous Cup Final, which I so very nearly missed.'

Word of the dynamic wing-half's performances for the Hoops had reached north of the border. In 1943, Belfast Celtic, one the great club sides on the island of Ireland, who had nurtured Jack Coulter before selling him on to Everton in 1934, were reportedly extremely keen to secure the Dalkey man's services. Clubs and players rarely spurned Celtic's advances but on this occasion, Rovers did not offer any encouragement to the Belfast side and had Peter sign on for another year.

Peter received his second call-up for the League of Ireland representative side in the annual game against Northern Ireland in March 1944. His opponent that day at inside-right for the North was the highly rated Jimmy McAlinden, who was later to become a teammate at Shamrock Rovers. McAlinden had built up quite a reputation for himself as an inside-forward and Peter was looking forward to one of his stiffest tests to date. In the event, he more than held his own against McAlinden in a 2–1 victory. In all, Peter would be selected seven times in Inter-League representative sides while with the Milltown outfit.

Following that Inter-League appearance against McAlinden, Peter formed the opinion that he would far rather mark a star player than come up against someone comparatively unknown:

> *In marking a star you are more apt to be on your toes for the full 90 minutes, because you know that you can't afford to relax for a moment, whereas when you play against a not so famous player you are sometimes inclined to give him less attention, which can prove fatal. Furthermore, if an outstanding inside-forward gives you the 'run around' you don't feel so badly about it, but if this happens from a very ordinary player it makes you look a poor performer indeed. The mere fact of having a more stylish and skilful opponent to face helps to pull that little extra capability out of you.*

Twelve months on from their FAI Cup victory in the spring of 1944, Rovers again reached the final of the same competition. This time there was no sore throat to worry Peter. The opponents (for only the second time in the national cup final) were North Dubliners Bohemians, so for the second successive year there would be a derby atmosphere. Rovers were victorious again but, by Peter's admission, there was a strong element of good fortune to the only goal of the match: 'The winning goal was a real fluke. Our centre-forward, Paddy Gregg, in attempting to volley a cross ball from outside-right Delaney, sliced it badly with the outside of his foot and it trickled slowly into the far corner of the net.' Little did Peter realise it at the time, but this would be his last winner's medal in senior football. The Hoops would also collect the Dublin City Cup and President's Cup that season.

Rovers reached a third successive FAI Cup final in 1946. Although his brother Jim and sister Sheila had watched him play on many occasions, his mother had never set eyes on him on the pitch. He was determined to get her to this final and used all of his persuasive powers to get her there. Her lifelong friend, Mr Kelly, promised to accompany her if she would go. A neighbour's offer to drive them the ten miles to the final sealed it. Mrs Farrell proved not to be a lucky mascot, however – the Milltown lads went down 1–2 to Drumcondra. When her son returned home after the game and asked how she had enjoyed it, she said, 'You had very hard luck, Peter, but I could have stayed there all day listening to the band.'

5
ENTERING THE INTERNATIONAL STAGE

With the disappointment of being unable to retain the cup a second time etched in the Shamrock Rovers players' minds, they sought to make amends by winning the 1946 Belfast and Dublin Inter-City Cup competition (the Inter-City Cup for short), which was, as its name indicated, competed for by the top clubs either side of the border in Ireland. It was played on a knock-out system basis, with two-legged ties.

Shamrock Rovers overcame Glentoran 4-3 in a hard-fought quarter-final second leg played in Belfast, on their way to meeting Distillery in the semi-final and Belfast Celtic in the final. Unbeknown to Peter and his teammate and friend Tommy Eglington, the pair had caught the eye of the watching Ernest Green and Theo Kelly – an Everton director and the club's secretary-manager. The pair had been over from Merseyside to scout Shelbourne's Eddie Gannon but, with a few hours to kill before their boat back, they also took in the evening match featuring Shamrock Rovers.

By his personal recollection, Peter had played 'out of my skin' in one of his best appearances in the green and white hoops. The Toffees were reigning Football League champions (from 1939, due to the war) but in desperate need of fresh blood. Ireland held the promise of talent not impacted by conflict and years of rationing –

and available for a modest fee.

As the squad awaited the arrival of the train to convey them to their base at Bangor, Messrs Kelly and Green stepped forward and asked Tommy and Peter how they could get in touch with the Shamrock Rovers board, with a view to securing their signatures for Everton. Peter duly gave Kelly the address of the Dublin club's chairman before boarding the train.

Having defeated Belfast Celtic away (3–1), Rovers clung on in the second leg at Dalymount Park after Charlie Tully had given the Northern Irish side hope with a second-half goal. As the final whistle sounded on that Thursday night, with Shamrock Rovers emerging victorious, 3-2 on aggregate, Peter was filled with a sense of elation, following several cup-competition near misses: 'It was certainly the greatest moment of my life, and I know from the look of the lads in the bath after the game that they were experiencing the same emotion. You can imagine the feeling of our team when we all realised that, at last, we had given our supporters some reward for the way they have stood by us through thick and thin.' He little realised that this was to be his last appearance in the green and white hooped shirt of Shamrock Rovers, the club he had joined as a schoolboy seven years previously.

While negotiations commenced between Everton and Shamrock Rovers, 23-year-old Peter was called up for senior international honours for the first time. It is worth, at this point, giving some background to the international game on the island of Ireland, which had two teams competing as 'Ireland'. The Belfast-based Irish Football Association (IFA) was formed in 1880 and was the organising body for the sport across all of the island of Ireland in the pre-partition days. It had been organising fixtures for the national team, playing as Ireland, since 1882 and it also oversaw the challenge cup competition.

Partition in 1921, in the wake of the Irish War of Independence (also known as the Anglo–Irish War), saw the island split in two. There would be six counties in the north, with a Protestant majority in the population, which remained, under the name Northern Ireland, as part of the home countries (and is part of the United Kingdom to this day). The 26 counties in the south, with an overwhelmingly Roman Catholic population, would first become known as the Irish Free State. It formally became a republic in 1949 and is known internationally and constitutionally as Ireland (Éire in Irish Gaelic).

The Football Association of Ireland (FAI) was founded in Dublin shortly after partition, with the intention of overseeing the sport in the 26 counties. The FAI did not automatically qualify for international status but, two years after its formation, it obtained recognition from FIFA, the world's governing body for football (albeit initially rebranded as the FA of the Irish Free State – FAIFS for short). The representative team of the FAI would first play competitively at the 1924 summer Olympics, held in Paris, and would go on to play, typically, once or twice a year against European opposition (never the home nations of the UK).

There were tensions between the FAI and IFA, as both believed they had some claim over football across the entire island. This would be reflected when it came to selecting players for their national teams. Post-partition, the IFA continued to field a national team, playing as Ireland, in the British Home Championship. It would regularly select a modest number of players from the south of the island, including Everton's Dublin-born forward Alex Stevenson.

The FAI side did not participate in the British Home Championship, instead arranging to play friendlies against mainland European sides. The matches away to Portugal and Spain in June 1946 would be the first official fixtures to be played by

The cap awarded to Peter for his international debut for Ireland (FAI) against Portugal in 1946 (credit: Devlin family)

A young supporter gets to wear the coveted cap

the national side since a match against Germany, played in Bremen, three months before the outbreak of the Second World War. As part of the arrangement, it was agreed that Portugal and Spain would make return visits to Dublin.

There is no doubt that Peter was selected by his country on merit, but it is fair to record that Rovers' players had the advantage of having club director Tom Scully as a permanent fixture on the selection committee. The FAI took full advantage of a thawing of the frosty relationship between the soccer associations in the north and south of the island of Ireland by calling on five players of Northern Irish birth, playing for either Northern Irish or English clubs (one would not travel due to a reluctance to fly). These would be the last fixtures in which the FAI fielded a combined 'North and South' side, but the Belfast-based IFA would continue to pick the best players from either side of the border in Ireland for several more years.

The Aer Lingus DC-3 flight to Lisbon, with a fuelling stop at Bordeaux en route, was Peter's first experience of flying, and his first trip beyond the British Isles. Mid-flight, he was stunned to be approached by Joe Wickham, secretary of the FAI, and advised that he would not only be making his debut but also captaining the side against Portugal. What seems like a bizarre decision may be explained by the selectors making a political point by giving the honour to a home-based player. Johnny Carey was the obvious choice, but he was employed by Manchester United and also had his hands full as coach of the squad. Also, Tom Scully probably pushed hard for recognition for his Rovers player. Given the shock captaincy news, Peter was dumbstruck: 'I was so thrilled at this thought that my mind could think of nothing else for the remainder of the journey, not even the fact that we were several thousand feet up in the sky. I went to bed in a Lisbon hotel that night still hardly able to believe the fact that I was to be captain was true.'

The young captain leads the Irish team onto the pitch in Madrid to face Spain for his second international appearance for the FAI

Ireland went down 1–3 to Portugal in Lisbon – they were three goals down in the Estadio Da Luz within 30 minutes – at which point centre-half Con Martin had to deputise in goal for the injured Ned Courtney. Remarkably, the stand-in, who had previously excelled at Gaelic football, did not concede any goals and remained in this role for the match against Spain at the Estadio Metropolitano de Madrid. Martin, who would make a number of appearances between the sticks for Aston Villa when there was an injury crisis, repeated his goalkeeping heroics in Madrid.

With Martin repelling the Spaniards' attempts on goal, Paddy Sloan, who had just moved from Tranmere Rovers to Arsenal, scored the only goal of the match. As the Irish team entered the pitch prior to kick-off, there was an almighty roar. A flabbergasted Peter turned to Johnny Carey to comment on it – whereupon the older man pointed out that the cheering coincided with the country's leader, General Franco, taking his seat in the stand, rather than it being a generous Iberian salute to the Irish players.

The coin toss had comedic value as the referee and two captains did not have a common language between them. Much gesturing and grunting was required to establish who had won the toss and in which direction the Irish would kick-off. The memorable trip ended with the presentation of international caps at Dublin's

Gresham Hotel. The nervous novice captain made his first ever public speech — which he later described as 'very brief indeed'.

Peter's character is encapsulated by what happened next. Rather than have his first cap mounted on his mantlepiece, he gave it to Christy Devlin, his coach at Cabinteely United, as a token of appreciation for the influence he'd had on his football career. The cap remains a prized possession of the Devlin family.

Prior to kick-off in his second Ireland appearance, Peter does the floral presentation and handshake with the Spanish team captain

An action shot from the match in Madrid in June 1946. General Franco was in attendance and witnessed an Irish victory

6
CROSSING THE IRISH SEA

Having touched down back in Ireland, Peter and Tommy Eglington were instructed to go to Mr and Mrs Cunningham's home the following evening to discuss the Everton approach for them. First, Peter took his souvenirs from Spain and Portugal to show his family, but thoughts quickly turned to the impending decision about his footballing future.

At the meeting *chez* Cunningham, it was explained to the pair that terms had been agreed with Everton. The formidable May Cunningham had negotiated fees of £2,000 for Peter and £1,000 for Tommy (erroneously reported in the press as totalling £10,000) – a friendly match between the sides at Goodison Park would also be scheduled. However, it was made clear that the ultimate decision rested with the two players. They were given a few days to reflect and come to a conclusion.

There were a good number of things for the pair to ponder about moving to another land. They had to be convinced about moving to a country enduring severe austerity and in a state of disrepair after six years of war. Liverpool was a particularly badly hit city. Furthermore, footballers' wages were capped and not everyone was welcoming to people coming from Ireland, a country that had remained officially neutral during the recent conflict. Peter would admit, candidly, some years later: 'I didn't want to go. I was too happy at home and with Rovers. I had no ambition.' He was also wary of failing to make the grade in England and having to return home as a 'failure'.

Strongly encouraged by his mother, he made the decision to join the Toffees, as did Tommy Eglington. It was not without a sense of trepidation, however. Some 36 years after the move, Peter reflected: 'My head was full of my Christian Brothers indoctrination which would have me believe England was the home of all evil.' The two Dubliners need not have worried about how life would be for them in this most Irish of English cities. Peter stated: 'I spent the best part of 16 years playing soccer in England and I never encountered any serious anti-Irish feeling. The people of Liverpool looked on me as favourably as one of their own.'

Don Kendall, writing as 'Pilot' for the *Liverpool Evening Express*, hailed the low-cost double-purchase by the Toffees: 'Personally, I think the masterstroke was to secure Farrell and Eglington from Shamrock Rovers, for it is no easy thing to get players to leave an area where there are no wages limits. It just shows what personality can do. Mr. Kelly succeeded where many others would have failed. Mr. Kelly has pursued a courageous policy, but I am confident that Everton will reap a rich reward.'

May Cunningham had told Pilot: 'You will find Peter and Tommy charming fellows and grand players.' Others had assured the Merseyside journalist that the pair would prove to be Ireland's finest football exports – no mean boast when Johnny Carey was plying his trade so successfully for Manchester United. Peter had tempered his expectations, recalling: 'I did not dare to hope of achieving any great prominence in the game. I felt I would be content if I could jog along, just making ends meet and perhaps putting a bit aside for the rainy day which all who earn their living at football must expect some time or another.'

The transfer forms were signed in the Gresham Hotel on 11 July 1946 in the presence of Joe Cunningham and Theo Kelly. Peter would confess to paying scant attention to the document being signed: 'You never had to look at the fine print on your contract. You

Peter and Tommy Eglington on board the boat that was taking them to Merseyside to begin their Everton careers in the summer of 1946 (credit: Eglington family)

just signed it in the confidence that it would be right and fair.'

On 28 July, Peter bade farewell to football on home soil by lining up for a 'Visitors' team boasting several international players in a friendly against the hosts Skerries United in the seaside town north of Dublin. The following day, the new Toffees pair were photographed boarding the vessel that would make the night crossing to Liverpool. Meeting the bleary-eyed and somewhat anxious Irishmen on the Mersey quayside were Theo Kelly, club captain Norman Greenhalgh – nicknamed Rollicker – and Alex Stevenson. Stevenson was a fellow Dubliner with a mix of Italian and Scottish heritage. Raised as a Protestant, he had starred for local side Dolphin before a transfer to Glasgow Rangers. Moving to Everton in 1934, the clever inside-forward, known by his colleagues as Stevie, had a well-earned reputation an inveterate practical joker – but he was also a superb footballer in the Alex James style in his pre-war pomp. Greenhalgh and Stevenson, both Football League Championship winners as Toffeemen in 1939, proved a great help in settling the Irish pals in their new surroundings.

After a visit to a café next to Goodison Park, there was a quick tour of the stadium. It was Peter's first visit to Everton's home ground, and he was suitably impressed: 'You can imagine the impression it left on me as I gazed out from the Directors' Box on this impressive-looking stadium encased by its massive double-decked stands.'

Peter and Tommy were then taken to their digs on Harris Drive, Bootle, in the care of Mrs Egan. The kind-hearted landlady became like a second mother to the pair in those early months on Merseyside. 'As soon as we entered the house and met the Egan family, I knew this was going to be a home from home. And so it proved during our five years' residence at this abode before I married. No woman could have done more for anyone than Mrs. Egan did for us, and I can assure you that I, and I know I am also speaking for Tommy, shall be forever grateful to the Egans for making us feel so welcome in such a happy environment.'

The pair both joined St Robert Bellarmine's CYMS (Catholic Young Men's Society) and, needless to relate, the members went out of their way to make the new arrivals feel at home. As regular churchgoers, their Christian (Roman Catholic) faith was important to Tommy and Peter. At some point during their time living in Liverpool, there were diminishing donations during church services to the collection plate, which funded the priest's accommodation and food. Knowing that other congregation members would follow the lead of the two local footballing celebrities, the priest hatched a plan. By prior arrangement, he had the pair each place a very generous offering in the collection plate when it was passed to them on the front row. Seeing this, other members of the congregation felt compelled to be more forthcoming with their cash than usual, reaping the priest a bumper financial harvest. Post-service, the priest surreptitiously refunded three-quarters of what Peter and Tommy had 'donated'.

A couple of months after arriving in England, Tommy wrote home to his parents to let them know how he and his compadre were settling in, and gave them reassurance that he was able to continue with his Catholic lifestyle:

Bootle, Liverpool

15/10/46

Dear Ma & Pa,

Just a few lines to let you know that I arrived back after my long journey. We left Liverpool at 5pm on Friday and we arrived in Newcastle at 10:30pm – we stayed there all the time – it was only a few miles from Sunderland. I slept with a Catholic – McIlhatton, the outside-right – and the two of us went to Mass.

We left Newcastle at 9:40 Sunday morning and arrived back in Liverpool at 4pm. It was a grand trip, and they can take a beating very well, the directors included. Well Pop, we were beaten badly – the team did not play as well as usual. I had a good game myself and scored a grand goal. Our outside-right sent in a high ball and the opposing centre-half headed it away. Before it hit the ground I smacked it into the net. It was the best goal that I ever scored, and all the lads gave me a great handshake after the match. They are the best fellas in the world, and I don't think there is a better club in England even though we are not doing too good. Sunderland have a great side and I would say that they are the best we have played so far.

Mum – I hope that you got the money I sent you. Have you made up your mind when you are coming over? I hope that it will be soon. Tell all the family I was asking for them…

Yours truly,

Tom

PS By the time you receive this letter we might be out on strike. If we do come out, Peter and I are going home.

Peter had arrived on Merseyside with a badly sprained ankle – an injury sustained a week before travelling to Liverpool. One report said it was a knock sustained in training with Rovers at Milltown; another put it down to an injury incurred on the tennis court. A third explanation, put forward by Peter in the early 1980s, was that he took a knock while having a kickabout with Scottish campers in Dalkey. Regardless of the cause, x-rays taken in Liverpool of the injured ankle confirmed that rest and recuperation were required. The specialist engaged by Everton, Mr McMurray, instructed Peter to sit out matches and training.

His first impression of seeing the Toffees in action in a pre-season match was not unsurprising – 'This football is faster than anything we have had in Ireland' – and he wondered if he could make the grade. He would observe wing-halves Stan Bentham, Joe Mercer and Gordon Watson in training and playing, taking the opportunity to analyse what was required in that position in the First Division. Jock Thomson, a fine wing-half who had captained Everton to the league crown in 1938/39, had become the club's first coach (as opposed to trainer) and he must have been a valuable source of advice for a player finding his feet in the number six shirt.

While incapacitated, the new Everton man missed out on a famous first encounter between the FAI (Ireland) side and England that was played at Dalymount Park on 30 September. Peter's Everton clubmates, Alex Stevenson and Tommy Eglington, were selected to play. The former showed the supporters what they had been missing in the 14 years since his last FAI appearance. Stevenson's prolonged omission had been a source of consternation for Irish football supporters as well as the player. Some believed, erroneously, it was down to the Protestant forward's reluctance to play for the Dublin-based association (he was selected and played for the Belfast-based IFA team). This was untrue and caused Stevenson some hurt. In fact, he was the victim of English teams being reluctant to release players for FAI duty, as the Sunday fixtures caused issues with travel and heightened the risk of fatigue and injury.

Back in the side, Stevenson pulled the strings and, on the hour mark, unleashed a shot which crashed against the crossbar – prompting England goalkeeper Frank Swift to blow a kiss at the woodwork. Watched by 31,988 through the Dalymount drizzle, Tom Finney sealed a narrow 1–0 win for the visitors with a late scrambled goal.

It would be late November, after a couple more visits to the specialist and several reserve-team outings, when Peter was deemed fit for Everton first-team duties. Manager Theo Kelly gave him the news when he called him into his office. With a 'good luck' pat on the back, he said, 'You are playing left-half against Stoke on Saturday.' Peter was thrilled until the penny dropped that the one and only Stanley Matthews was to be on the right wing for the opposition. Peter later recalled that as the referee's bell rang for the side to take the field, all except one teammate offered encouragement and handshakes. As they headed for the pitch, Alex Stevenson, so often a wind-up merchant, reassured his compatriot that the Blues' left-back would deal with the famous winger.

The Dalkey man emerged from the Victoria Ground with credit, 'Stork' in the *Daily Post* commenting: 'Farrell made a satisfying debut. Strong in tackle, he also has an eye for a pass.' After the final whistle he felt a hand on his shoulder and turned to see none other than Stanley Matthews, who said, 'Well played, boy.' Then, in his own quiet unassuming way, the Stoke hero asked how Peter was getting on at Goodison Park. A simple gesture in itself, but one that Peter never forgot.

Peter's ascension to the first team helped to confirm to the directors that the injury-hampered Joe Mercer was surplus to requirements. After a brief stand-off with the club, during which he ran a Wirral grocery shop with his wife, the highly decorated England international departed for Arsenal. There, the former England star proved that he was far from finished in the game, winning silverware and playing into the mid-1950s. The Everton wing-half pairing in the mid-to-late 1940s would be selected from Peter, Stan Bentham, Gordon Watson and, subsequently, Cyril Lello. T.G. Jones or his Welsh compatriot Jack Humphreys occupied the central berth in the half-back line.

It didn't take long for the Irishman to rekindle the rapport with Tommy Eglington on the left side of the pitch that had been enjoyed at Shamrock Rovers. Clubmate Tom Gardner recalled: 'Peter and Tommy were good. Tommy seemed to know what Peter was going to do with that ball, knew exactly where it was going to go. It was fast, it was good football. Not the speed we've got today, but more direct. There was very little of the back-passing. Harry Cooke [the trainer] used to say, "Don't pass back unless you've got to!"'

In November 1946 Peter, along with compatriots Tommy Eglington and Alex Stevenson, added IFA honours to those of the Dublin-based FAI, when selected to play for the national team against Scotland in Glasgow. The Dalkey man would make seven appearances for the IFA from 1946–49. Of the occasion in Glasgow, he recalled:

> *I had heard quite a lot about the famous ground and its even more famous 'Hampden Roar', but both exceeded all my expectations. There were 100,000 spectators at Hampden Park on this Wednesday afternoon in 1946. I find it very hard to describe the volcanic roar that greeted the Scots as they took the field. This roar was repeated each time they threatened danger to the Irish goal and was rather a new experience for me, although the Goodison and Kop fans, in recent years, would hold their own with it.*

Once settled in the Everton side, Peter earned his spurs with his trademark wholehearted displays (29 that season) as he adjusted to life at the pinnacle of the English game:

> *The weeks of my first season seemed to fly with each week the renewed thrill of taking the field among such exalted company and the experience and honour of being in opposition to star inside forwards such as Mannion, Carter and Doherty. During the summer season of 1947 when I returned on holiday to my native Dalkey, many were the questions fired at me from the locals regarding English teams, and I also had to answer quite a few questions concerning the facilities of all the First Division grounds.*

His first taste of Merseyside derby action came in a 1–0 home win on 29 January 1947. The intensity of feelings on and off the pitch even got to the usually unflappable Farrell: 'As a rule, I never became nervous before a game, be it a cup match, an international or a league match. But I will confess that I always felt a little unnerved by those Liverpool derbies.' Nerves aside, Peter stuck to his task, drawing praise from Don Kendall in the *Evening Express*: 'Farrell had no superior in the close dribbling and tenacity of tackle.'

Although Everton may have been on a downward trajectory, Peter came to appreciate the status of the club and the importance of the personnel that made it tick:

> *During the early years at Goodison Park, I was beginning to learn one of the reasons why the name of Everton is respected everywhere, namely the homely spirit that prevails, and always has prevailed. I should like to mention one of the men mainly responsible for this, the evergreen Harry Cooke. Nothing has ever been too difficult to Harry in his help and assistance to players. Furthermore, Harry has made himself loved not only by the players, but by all visitors who have dropped in to have a look at Goodison Park. Despite his many duties, he has always found time to show these people around and explain everything in detail to them. It would make old Harry blush to hear the compliments paid him by some of these people. Long may he continue at Goodison, as it is hard to imagine Everton without Harry Cooke.*

7
TOFFEES TRIBULATIONS

Although it had been a source of satisfaction for Peter to pass muster in the English top flight, 1946/47 had been a disappointing campaign for the reigning league champions of 1939. It was made all the more draining by being played through Britain's Big Freeze, which began in mid-December and continued into March, going down as one of the harshest and snowiest winters on record. The impact on the fixture programme, in an age before undersoil heating, was immense, with Everton not completing their programme until 31 May.

With some players now long in the tooth, and the firepower of the departed Tommy Lawton sorely missed, the Blues had to settle for a tenth-place position, 14 points adrift of champions Liverpool. Just two players had reached double figures in goals: youth product Eddie Wainwright and Ephraim 'Jock' Dodds. Dodds, a burly number nine, who had, like Peter and Tommy Eglington, joined the Toffees from Shamrock Rovers. The Scot's transfer, however, was complicated by Blackpool FC holding his English League registration. It took considerable powers of negotiation by Theo Kelly, and payments made to both the Irish and Fylde coast clubs to bring the Scot to Merseyside. In the end, Everton had to shell out just shy of three times the fee paid for Peter and Tommy to secure Dodds' services, even though he was 31, such was their desperation to secure the services of a centre-forward with a proven scoring record. Three years later, Dodds, an enterprising character, become one of Britain's first football agents, acting on behalf of the Millonarios club of Bogota to tempt players to ply their trade in Columbia. Having acted without authority of the football authorities, he was punished by a ban from the sport in 1950. Peter was back in the FAI fold for the return fixtures against Spain and Portugal, played in March

The Everton squad photographed at Goodison Park in August 1947, prior to the start of Peter's second season with the Toffees (credit: Brendan Connolly collection)

and May 1947, respectively. The Spain match, in front of a record home gate of 42,102 saw a 3–2 win for the hosts. Con Martin would tell sportswriter Sean Ryan that an added attraction of being selected for the Irish home fixtures was the opportunity to get decent meal: 'It was our chance to eat something substantial for a change. With rationing still in force in England ... a trip home, where food was plentiful, had great appeal.'

The 1947/48 season was worse for Everton. With precious little fresh talent of note being acquired, this was a team destined for mediocrity, or worse. The 40 points accrued only secured a 14th-place finish, salt being rubbed in the wound for the Toffees faithful as revitalised Everton cast-off Joe Mercer inspired Arsenal to the title. The Blues' 52-goal haul in the league was 10 shy of that achieved in the previous season. Jock Dodds, with 13, was the only player to make it into double figures. Peter – never prolific – got off the mark as an Everton player with two goals from wing-half (he was frequently switched between right- and left-half). Coach Jock Thomson's

34

THE LIFE AND TIMES OF PETER FARRELL

Stretches at Everton's training ground, Bellefield, for Peter, Jock Dodds and Gordon Dugdale. Dugdale's promising career was ended by a heart condition.

Peter and Tommy in the Belfast-based IFA Ireland side in 1948, before a match against Wales.

departure to manage Manchester City in October 1947 would be keenly felt, with nobody stepping in with his level of football experience and tactical expertise.

A rare bright spot for Peter came on international duty when the Belfast-based Irish (IFA) side came to play England at Goodison Park in a British Home Championship match on 5 November 1947. Peter and Tommy found themselves (along with four other players who had also represented the FAI Ireland side) facing an England side boasting a formidable forward line of Matthews, Mortenson, Lawton, Mannion and Finney. Drawing on it being Bonfire Night, a match report

The Ireland team about to take on Spain in Barcelona in May 1948. Johnny Carey captains the side. Both Peter and Everton clubmate Alex Stevenson were making their sixth appearance for the FAI side, the latter having had a gap of 14 years between his debut and next selection.

described the thrilling match, watched by 67,980 shoe-horned into the stadium, as 'explosive'. After a goalless first half, Davy Walsh had given the Irishmen a shock lead. Mannion and Lawton responded in the final ten minutes to put England ahead but, in the dying seconds, Peter Doherty of Huddersfield Town launched himself at an Eglington cross to head the equaliser. With the scorer still lying prone on the ground, the final whistle was blown – giving Ireland its first point against England after 12 unsuccessful attempts spread over 20 years. One report hailed Peter, along with John Vernon, Peter Doherty and Bill Walsh, as 'the cornerstones of a fine team performance by the Irish'. The *Northern Whig* newspaper hailed it as 'the most dramatic finish ever seen in an international game'.

A match-up between Peter's present and former employers came to pass in the festive period of 1947. The fixture, a day after the Toffees' Boxing Day home win over Sunderland in the league, was an ideal opportunity to give Peter the captaincy. He led the Blues to a convincing 7–0 victory over Shamrock Rovers, with Jock

Peter, with Blues clubmates Eddie Wainwright and Wally Fielding, obliging young fans asking for autographs (credit: Wainwright family)

Dodds netting a hat-trick. A *Daily Post* preview of the match noted that, in light of the cordial negotiations over the transfers of Dodds, Farrell and Eglington, the Blues had first refusal on any Rovers players they fancied bringing to Goodison Park.

A few weeks after the Shamrock Rovers match, Peter was in the wars against Derby County. Stretchered off in the final minute at Goodison Park, checks confirmed that the captain had sustained a fractured jaw, a badly split lip which required stitches, and extensive dental damage. Notwithstanding the injuries, he was keen to get back playing and even travelled with the squad to the Midlands hotel they were staying in before the subsequent match, against Wolves at Molineux. Only on the morning of the game was the prudent decision taken to give the jaw more time to heal, but he was back in the thick of it a mere three weeks after the bruising incident.

That season he found himself again alternating between the left and right wing-half positions as the struggling side was chopped and changed in search of a winning formula. Two years on from his FAI debut, Peter returned to the Iberian peninsula for fixtures against Portugal and Spain, coming away empty-handed.

The Everton club captaincy formally passed to Peter in the summer of 1948 – recognition of the leadership qualities he had demonstrated in difficult circumstances.

THE EMERALD EVERTONIAN

Heading practice with Eric Moore, Eddie Wainwright and Tommy Eglington on the small training ground, located between the Bullens Road and Park End stands.

Head tennis doubles – no prizes for correctly guessing who Peter has partnered with

38

He had been deputising as skipper for much of the previous season for left-back Norman Greenhalgh, who was struggling to shake off an ankle injury. Stork, in the *Liverpool Echo*, felt it was richly deserved and a wise appointment: 'He has all the attributes needed to make a successful skipper; particularly the dogged spirit and whole-heartedness which can inspire his colleagues to fight back when the tide is running against them.' Unsurprisingly, Tommy Eglington wholeheartedly approved of the honour for this close friend. 'Peter was an excellent reader of the game with a good sense of humour. Very forceful, he was an honest-to-goodness player and all of those assets made him a natural leader,' was his reflection several decades later.

Ball work at Bellefield. In the middle is T.G. Jones, the talismanic centre-half who briefly replaced Peter as club captain in 1949. Jones would leave Everton in 1950 to manage a Pwllheli hotel

Eglington's and Stork's assessments tallied with the observations of William Barrington Hill, a supporter who had been a regular on the Gwladys Street terrace since his first match in 1942, at the age of ten: 'Peter always played with a smile on his face but wherever he went, you knew he was captain. He was an excellent example of one, and the players obviously looked up to him. He was barrel-chested but very much a 90-minutes player who led by example. He had good ball control and was a very strong tackler – aggressive but not dirty.'

The award of the club captaincy followed some bizarre rumours that the wing-half was looking to forgo soccer and train for the priesthood. He asked the *Liverpool Echo* to put out a statement denying the fanciful rumour, confirming instead that his only preparation for the future, post-playing, was to study for quantity surveying at some point.

Perhaps the closest Peter and his great friend Tommy Eglington came to being ordained was turning out in a football team of priests in Liverpool. Father John Ashton told James Corbett, author of *Faith of Our Families*, 'Peter and Tommy were very good Catholics, and they were very pally with us priests. As priests we had a [football] team and, for a while, I was captain. Farrell and Eglington used to play with us!'

The award of the captaincy coincided with an extremely difficult start to the 1948/49 season – just two wins in 12 matches. Belatedly, the club moved to appoint its first manager with full control of team affairs. Theo Kelly had been a very capable club secretary before the war but struggled with the dual role of secretary-manager

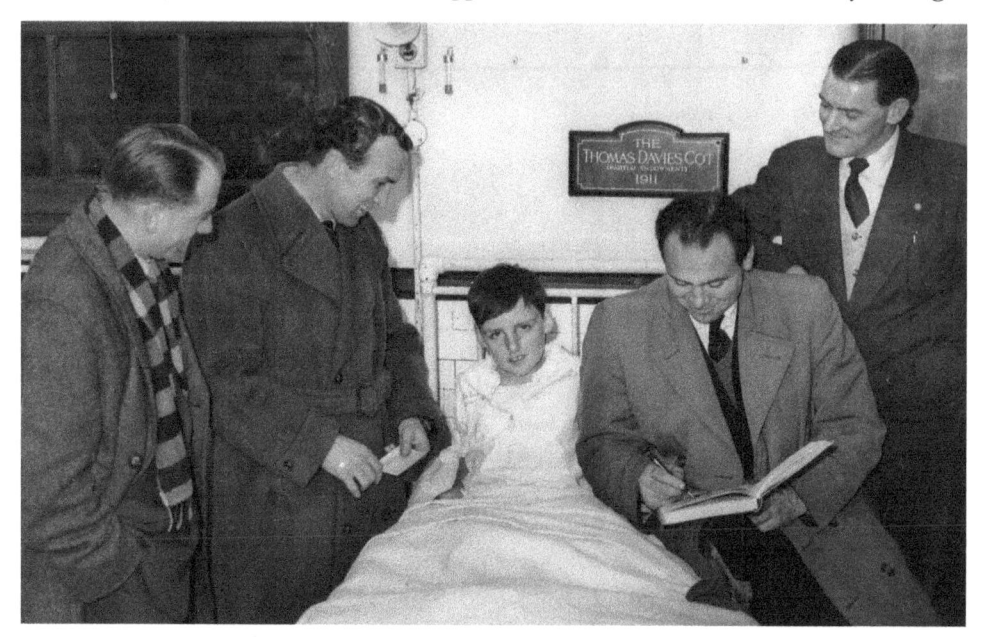

Peter took his responsibilities to the local community in Liverpool seriously. Here, along with Eddie Wainwright and Tommy Eglington, he visits a child in hospital

and was not in the rudest of health. In a move that would be repeated several times in later decades, the club turned to a former player for salvation.

Cliff Britton, a cultured wing-half for the Toffees throughout the 1930s, had rapidly made a name for himself in management during the immediate post-war years. In spite of a modest budget, the Bristolian had led Burnley to promotion and an FA Cup final in 1946/47. With only 32 league goals conceded, the back line had been topically dubbed 'The Iron Curtain' in a nod to Winston Churchill's quote about the Soviet Union. The following season saw the Clarets finish third in the top flight, so it was little surprise that Britton was high on the Blues' wish-list. He was tempted back to his first footballing love, on the proviso that he had unfettered control over first-team affairs. Theo Kelly reverted to a purely administrative role, before leaving in the early 1950s due to his worsening health issues.

The new man at the helm was keen to establish his authority. He insisted on being addressed as Mr Britton, even by former teammates like Norman Greenhalgh and T.G. Jones, who took umbrage at this. In an unpublished memoir, unseen until 2024, he outlined his approach to managership:

> *It is not only necessary to have this authority to do the job but for the manager to hold the respect of the players. If they get to know that he lacks the power to enforce his own instructions he can expect a rough passage. To receive the full cooperation of the players the manager's first action is to establish himself as THE BOSS. None of his staff should have any doubts about that. One can't get the full cooperation of the players by just telling them what to do.*

His firm yet fair approach and tactical acumen saw the Toffees steered away from the rocks of relegation – but it was a close call. The 37 points garnered from 42 matches (with two points for a win) saw the Blues finish in 18th place, four points clear of the drop zone.

It was a proud honour to captain the club, but in such difficult circumstances on the pitch, the club felt that it had weighed heavily on the Irishman and affected his form and judgement. Peter, looking back, disputed that, feeling that his dip in form was unrelated to the captaincy and merely one of those things a footballer experiences at some point in his career. Nonetheless, with the humiliation of relegation avoided, Britton sought to take some pressure off Peter and made T.G. Jones skipper for 1949/50, in recognition of the classy but often unsettled centre-half's resurgent form after a move to Roma fell through. As vice-captain, Peter would lead the team once Jones – out of form and at odds with Britton – was dropped for good over the festive period. With great pride, he retained the mantle of club captain for the rest of his days at Goodison Park. Jones, meanwhile, would seek new pastures as a hotelier and player-manager of Pwllheli and District FC.

Peter had rounded off the 1948/49 season with fixtures against Portugal and Spain at Dalymount. The players benefitted from some extended time training together – a novelty – and defeated the former 1–0. The victory saw the first deployment of a substitute at home by the FAI when Peter was brought on for the injured David Walsh in the 35th minute. However, he was taken back off just four minutes later when the patched-up Walsh returned to the fray. Despite being buoyed by the win over Portugal, the Irish were no match for a superb attacking side which, benefitting from hot conditions, romped to a 4–1 victory after falling behind to an Irish spot kick.

It was around this time that a young John McFarlane was getting his first tastes of watching the Blues at Goodison Park. Peter's wholehearted displays in what we would now term midfield left a lasting impression on the boy: 'People around the country might say, 'Who was Peter Farrell?' Well, he wasn't a Wilf Manion or Len Shackleton, but he was an inspiration. He was a superb captain; I rate him to be the best I have seen at Goodison – and there have been one or two decent ones. He was an inspiration. He never stopped, he put himself about and was a bit of an enforcer, for want of a better word. He'd gee everyone up. He'd come off the pitch in the middle of winter with sweat dripping off him.'

Another young Evertonian was Ron Tennant, who would cycle up with schoolfriends from their homes in Speke, at the south end of the city, to watch the players do pre-season training. He recalled how he could get up close to the squad: 'The training always took the form of running from Goodison down the East Lancs Road, around Broadway and along Queens Drive back to Goodison. Peter Farrell used to give me money to buy oranges and other fruit for the players to eat when they got back to Goodison. I was one of only a few lads allowed to watch the players train in the far corner of the Park End. Happy days; thanks for the memories, Peter.'

The accessibility of the stars of Merseyside football in this era is highlighted in what Everton supporter Gerry Moore subsequently told author James Corbett:

> *I remember one day I got off the bus at Spellow Lane and I went to buy some sweets in a shop on the corner of one of the streets that lead down to County Road. As I got in there, Peter Farrell was in there buying some cigarettes [ed. pipe tobacco, is more likely]. I was surprised to see him, but I got chatting to him. He actually waited for me to buy my sweets and then chatted to me as we walked to the ground and then he went into the players' entrance. You would never get that happening now!*

A further example of the Irishman's willingness to connect with supporters was given by Joan Foster (née Smyth) when interviewed by an Everton Collection oral history project in 2010:

> *'Every day of my life at St Michael's school on West Derby I wore my Everton scarf. One day when I was ten, my teacher Mr McGrory said, "Miss Smyth, a friend of yours is coming, so don't leave when school ends at half past three. I said, "Why sir?" "Never mind why," he replied. So, the next thing I am standing there with my Everton scarf on and who walks in but Peter Farrell. I was so excited. Mr McGrory said, "This is my friend Peter Farrell. I have told him a heck of a lot about you and how you go to the games." The next think, Peter took the scarf from my neck, put it around his and literally put me on his shoulders for a few minutes, walking around the classroom.*
>
> *I went home, I was so excited and told my dad about it and he went, "Hmm, yes ok." You don't believe me dad, do you?" Then my dad went over to the local church, St Michael's, to organise a family funeral. When he came back, he said, "I have just been talking to Father and he said, "What's this about Peter Farrell having your daughter on his shoulders?" And I said, "Do you believe me now, Dad?!"*

8
GREENS TRIUMPH AT THE HOME OF THE BLUES

It was during the 1949/50 season, bitterly disappointing at club level with only 34 points accrued and 42 goals scored, that Peter enjoyed a brace of career highlights. On Christmas Eve, he lined up at inside-right forward in the Merseyside derby at Anfield. Sensationally, he scored after just 15 seconds, as described for the *Evening Express* by Don Kendall:

> From Wainwright to Powell and then Wainwright ran in inside-left to draw Hughes and four yards outside the penalty area slipped the ball square along the floor to his right for Farrell to run in at top pace and crack a glorious foot shot into the top corner of the net. Such was the force of the shot, which literally flashed by the diving Sidlow that it struck the iron net support and bounced right back into play. Farrell gave a whoop of delight as he was smothered by his colleagues.

It was the scorer's misfortune that this sensational strike in enemy territory was overshadowed by the Reds' three goals in reply.

However, Peter's finest and most famous moment at Goodison Park came three months before that Merseyside derby – and it was in the green of Ireland rather than the royal blue of Everton. The Irish side (formally billed as a Football Association

Ireland XI) was to play England at Everton's stadium on Wednesday 21 September.

Talks had begun in February 1949 between the English FA and the FAI; the minutes of the FAI International Affairs Committee give us a window into the prolonged back and forth required to get the show on. The FA's international committee had moved to invite the Irish team over and suggested Liverpool as a

The Everton team in 1949. Peter Corr, far left on the front row, would appear with Peter for Ireland at Goodison Park in September of that year

suitable city. In reply to Stanley Rous's letter, the FAI welcomed the invitation and the proposal that the match be played on Merseyside, due to its sea links to Ireland. It added that a midweek game on 21 September would be preferable; kick-off would be at 3pm, the absence of floodlights making an evening kick-off impractical. With a date agreed, the FA confirmed Goodison Park as the venue.

The FAI fully expected a mass exodus of Irish sports fans to Goodison and in July made contact with British Railways and the B&I Steampacket Company about possible supporters' deals for the boat trip to Liverpool. The officials of the Irish party itself would travel by boat, with Oscar Traynor, the FAI president and elected member of the Dáil Éireann (Irish parliament), leading the official delegation.

It was not all plain sailing with the arrangements, however, as the thorny issue of what the Irish team should be referred to had to be grasped. FAI Secretary Joe Wickham wrote to Stanley Rous to complain about the designation of the game as one between England and Éire, as in all previous international games they had played under the title of Ireland. Rous explained that he was keen to avoid confusion with the IFA side, which played under the moniker Ireland in the British Home Championship. He came up with the compromise of advertising the game as one between England and the FA of Ireland.

Wickham enlisted the help of Everton's secretary Theo Kelly in reserving the necessary hotel accommodation. The Prince of Wales Hotel in Southport was the first choice but when it transpired that the English FA had already booked it, a stay at the Palace Hotel in nearby Birkdale was arranged.

Notwithstanding the 2–2 draw with England earned by the IFA side at the same venue two years earlier, few gave the Irishmen much hope of victory. Peter himself was realistic about the likely outcome, but nonetheless happily had wagers with several clubmates that Ireland would pull off a shock.

The rather threadbare Irish squad had a session on Everton's training pitch the day before the big game and Joe Wickham came over to apologise to the Theo Kelly (who, in spite of his surname, was of Manx rather than Irish heritage) for selecting Peter at inside-right rather than wing-half. His rationale was that Peter would offer more weight and vim to the front line and offer support to clubmate Peter Corr, who would wear the green number seven shirt. The shock for supporters was the omission of Tommy Eglington, who was devastated not to be chosen to represent his country on his home club ground. Most thought Peter's great friend, a regular pick for a big-city club, would be an automatic choice, but the so-called Big Five panel of selectors thought otherwise. It seems that panel member Tom Scully used his influence to get Tommy O'Connor and Tommy Goodwin (both of Scully's Shamrock Rovers) into the team. Club chairman Joe Cunningham was reportedly less than impressed when Scully conveyed the news that two of his side would be travelling to England, thereby

The Ireland side which consigned England to its first home defeat by a foreign side. Captain Johnny Carey devised the successful gameplan. Tommy Eglington was unfortunate to miss out on the momentous occasion

Goodison Park viewed from the Bullens Road stand, probably during the match between England and Ireland

messing up his team selection plans.

Only seven players turned up for a training session the afternoon before the big game. Peter and Peter Corr were recuperating after training with Everton earlier in the day, while the likes of Con Martin and Davy Walsh were en route from their club commitments with Aston Villa and West Bromwich Albion respectively. Martin, along with many of the squad, saw a magician perform at the team hotel that evening, and mused that they needed a touch of the supernatural at Goodison the next day. On the bus to the ground, after lunch at Liverpool's Adelphi hotel, Martin told Peter that they would do well to concede four goals or less.

The press photo corps shared Con Martin's view on the likely match outcome when they chose which end to set up their cameras at. After the coin toss, all but one of the dozen or so lensmen headed for the Irish goal at the Gwladys Street End. The outlier, as he walked along the touchline towards the hosts' goal, was reportedly the recipient of light-hearted barracking from the terraces, along the lines of: 'Miracles only happen at Lourdes, what are you heading there for?!'

The Irish game plan, brilliantly devised by Johnny Carey, was to defend deep and stifle service to the home team's principal dangerman, Tom Finney. Irish players, notably Everton's two Peters, were tasked with blocking the line of sight for passing along the ground to Preston North End's star forward. England, instead, would have to loft passes, with much diminished effect. It worked a treat. The Irish took a shock lead on the 33rd minute when Peter Desmond (of Middlesbrough) was felled in the box and Con Martin blasted a penalty straight at goalkeeper Bert Williams, the sheer force of the strike carrying it over the line. For much of the rest of the match it was a rearguard action, but the men in green were steadfast in resisting the waves of England attacks. Then, with less than ten minutes remaining, Peter was put through on goal by Tommy O'Connor. As he advanced, he lofted the ball over Williams and, to the considerable

The cap from the famous defeat of England in 1949

delight of the many Merseysiders of Irish descent in the crowd, saw it nestle in the back of the Gwladys Street net. A justifiably proud Peter would eventually get to see the brief match highlights, including his goal at the Gwladys Street End, some years later. Described as a 'cute lob' in one report, a self-deprecating Peter would modestly say, 'I closed my eyes and banged it.'

Peter's strike completed the scoring. On the full-time whistle, he did a victory salute in the direction of his Toffees teammates sat in the stand, relishing the thought of collecting his £6 in wager winnings. As he put it himself with a glint in his eye, 'I won a lot of money from the Everton boys, although I seem to remember it took me a long time to collect it.'

The defeat at the hands of the 'Mighty Magyars' of Hungary in 1953 has often been, erroneously, cited as England's first defeat on home soil by a foreign nation, but Goodison Park four years earlier was the actual location and date of this sporting landmark. W.P. Murphy, the noted Irish sports journalist, proclaimed: 'The British Lion was in [a] sorry state last night. His den has been invaded, and his tail has been twisted by the FAI.'

Many messages of congratulation were received by the FAI in the wake of the monumental win. Joe Wickham ordered a copy of the souvenir page from the *Liverpool Echo*, which he intended to have framed and displayed at FAI headquarters in Merrion Square, Dublin. He also had a cheque for £3,169 8s 11d to cash – a 50 per cent share of the gate receipts.

The match has, with justification, become part of Irish sporting folklore; in 1974 the team was brought back together at an event staged in a Dublin hotel to mark the 25th anniversary of the shock result. Only Willie Walsh, who had emigrated to Australia, was absent, but Tommy Eglington deputised for him at the event.

The 1950 World Cup qualifying campaign for the Republic of Ireland (a name

Tommy and Peter packing for a foreign footballing trip to Scandinavia

that would be adopted in lieu of the Irish Free State) got underway on 2 June 1949 with a 3–1 defeat to Sweden in Stockholm and a September home victory over Finland. Having been overlooked for both fixtures, Peter was reinstated to the team for the 1–1 draw away to Finland in October, a last-minute goal from the hosts cancelling out Peter's first goal in the competition. For the qualifier against Sweden at Dalymount the following month, in an unusual act of largesse, the FAI had chartered a plane to take a number of Irish players from Liverpool to Dublin after their Saturday domestic matches. Unfortunately, the aircraft was grounded for a considerable time, meaning the Anglo-Irish players were exhausted when they kicked off on the Sunday afternoon in Dublin. Unsurprisingly, it was a comfortable victory for the Scandinavians, seemingly ending FAI interest in the competition.

The fielding of four players from the Republic for both the FAI and IFA in World Cup qualifying matches brought to a head the tensions arising from players being selected by both of the island's football organisations. Shamrock Rovers' owner Joe Cunningham wrote to players from the Republic, asking them to decline invitations to represent the Belfast-selected team, precipitating an end to the practice. Thus, Peter's IFA career was halted after his seventh cap, awarded for his appearance against Wales in March 1949.

Having failed to qualify for the 1950 World Cup finals to be staged in Brazil, the FAI received a telegram out of the blue in the spring of that year. It enquired if the Association would be prepared to send an Irish side take part in the finals, in the event of a vacancy arising. A round of committee meetings led to the conclusion that participation in a competition staged 6,000 miles away had the potential to bankrupt the body. Thus, a polite message declining the offer was sent, on the (fictitious) grounds of lack of time to prepare. As it was, only 13 of the 16 slots were filled at the finals and all participants made a healthy profit. It was a great opportunity missed for the young nation and its footballers.

One budding Irish footballer inspired by watching Peter and co. pulling on the green jersey at Dalymount was John Giles. The son of a Bohemians, Shelbourne and Distillery inside-forward, he would accompany his father, Dickie, to international fixtures. In his memoir, he'd recall the thrill of watching his homespun heroes – Carey, Coad, Walsh, Ringstead, Fitzsimons, Martin, Eglington and Farrell – take on foreign opponents. Giles would follow many of these across the sea, serving Manchester United, Leeds United and West Bromwich Albion with distinction and earning 59 caps.

When home in Ireland for the close season, Peter and Tommy Eglington, as two of the country's highest-profile football stars, would be co-opted to appear in the series of *Crackpots* football matches. Staged predominantly at Dalymount, these fun fixtures – full of farce and high jinks – drew huge crowds, with the gate receipts going towards supporting local children's hospitals. The sides comprised the Crackpots, a side from the entertainment business, and the Inkblots, from the sporting press. A smattering of Irish sporting stars was added to the mix and, on at least one occasion, Peter and Tommy captained the rival teams.

9
LOVE MATCH

Tommy Eglington had dated Doris 'Dorrie' O'Donohue before tying the knot with her in Dublin in the summer of 1950. Unsurprisingly, he turned to Peter to perform the best man duties. On returning to Liverpool, the newlyweds lodged for several months with Tommy's former landlady Mrs Egan in Bootle until moving into a club house on Mostyn Avenue in Old Roan (not far from where a future Everton star, Derek Temple, would run a Post Office following his retirement from playing in the 1970s). In time, they raised three children, Bernard, Anthony and Paula.

Back in 1946, Peter had first encountered Mabel Carney at a dance in the Cliff Castle, Dalkey. He had arrived at the function after a Sunday game; they had a couple of dances and then parted company. They didn't meet again until 1949, when Peter was home from Liverpool for the summer holidays; at this point the romance blossomed.

Mabel had been born on 22 September 1928 in New York to Irish parents Ernest

Carney and his wife Elizabeth (née Kavanagh), who had emigrated to the USA, Mabel's father being in the building trade. The Great Crash of 1929 changed everything, so the family made plans to move back to Ireland. Mabel's paternal aunt was Winifred 'Winnie' Carney, a remarkable woman, born and raised in Belfast, who had been very active in the Irish independence movement. In 1916 she was arrested and imprisoned for her part in the Easter Rising at the Dublin General Post Office. She was James Connolly's adjutant and one of only three females in the GPO on that day. It is said that she came armed with a Webley revolver and a typewriter. The latter was put to good use, typing out the Proclamation of Independence. Winnie was involved in the suffragist movement and, as a staunch socialist, worked for much of her life in the trade union movement. Notably, she actively campaigned for improved working conditions for women working in Northern Irish linen mills.

Ironically, given her background, Winifred fell in love with a Belfast Orangeman and former Ulster Volunteer and First World War veteran called George McBride. Clearly, this was a case of 'love conquers all'. The pair married in a civil ceremony in Holyhead, Wales, as there was little support for the romantic relationship from their respective families. She had accommodated her nieces and nephews, including Mabel and daughter-in-law Elizabeth, in Belfast on their return from New York. This arrangement lasted for a year or two until such time as her brother, Ernest, had secured the funds to set up his new family home in the Dublin area. Having lived

Peter and Mabel on their wedding day, 27 June 1951.
The couple honeymooned in Galway before setting up home in Litherland.

The inseparable Irish friends modelling their international caps

Mabel Farrell and Dorrie Eglington get a turn with their husbands' caps

with ill health for some years, this remarkable woman passed away in 1943 at the age of 55; George would live until 1988. To coincide with International Women's Day in 2024, a statue of Winifred was unveiled outside Belfast City Hall. It depicted her in a 1916 Citizen Army uniform, accompanied, naturally, by her typewriter and a Webley revolver.

Tall and sporty, Mabel Carney would play tennis with Peter in the Beeches Tennis Club in Dún Laoghaire. Mabel later recalled her future husband as being very handsome and great fun to be with. Although they only saw each other during the holidays, and when she visited him the odd time in Liverpool, she knew he was the one for her.

The couple married on 27 June 1951 at St Michael's Church in Dún Laoghaire. The bride was dressed in pale blue organdie, with a red bouquet, and among the guests were compatriots and Everton teammates Tommy Eglington, Jimmy O'Neill, Don Donovan, John Sutherland and George Cummins – also there was Peter's Ireland teammate Con Martin. The newlyweds honeymooned in Salthill, Galway, before setting up the marital home at 17 Thirlmere Drive, Litherland, a quiet backwater in close proximity to the busy road linking Seaforth with Southport (A5036). As with most Everton players' families in this era, they could not afford to buy a house outright, instead renting the semi-detached property from the club, who had purchased it for £1,800. In 1954 the rate payable was 25 shillings (£1.25) per week. In the hallway was one of the most prized wedding presents of the Farrells – a modest little ornament from the choirboys of Dalkey, who saved up for it and presented it to their football hero as a mark of appreciation of the many times he had addressed them.

At first, Mabel found life Liverpool lonely at times. Her new husband would be training at Goodison Park and Bellefield, travelling to away fixtures or making an enthusiastic contribution to local organisations – he was a great ambassador for the sport, giving talks to many clubs and community bodies around the city. So, she would be on her own for much of the time. Nonetheless, she would form a deep affinity for the city and its people.

The pair made great friends during their time in England and were blessed with wonderful neighbours. One summer, while Mabel was back visiting Ireland and Peter was away on a tour, she had the living room decorated. Not looking forward to putting things back in order on her return, she was astounded to find that in the wake of decorators, the house was as clean as a new pin. It transpired that her neighbours on either side got together and not only cleaned up everywhere, but had washed the curtains, put them back and prepared meal for her and the two children. One kind-hearted Samaritan had even had a large Indian carpet dry-cleaned and relaid! Not to be outdone by the women, the menfolk had kept the grass and hedges trimmed and, knowing that Peter was away for nearly a month, had put bedding

The Farrells plus young neighbour Pat Laverty captured at home for a newspaper article

plants in the borders. Tommy Eglington's wife Dorrie became a very close friend – a bond that would endure after their return to Ireland in the 1960s.

Peter and Mabel loved greyhound racing – every Thursday night they used to go to watch it at the Stanley Park track. Another favourite for Mabel was an excursion to Blackpool, where she would get on anything that moved fast and high – leaving Peter standing with his feet firmly planted on the ground, watching and worrying while she went on all the rides. Peter's interests were more sedate, his stated ambition being to get his golf handicap down to single figures from 14 – his quest was helped by Bootle Golf Club being within sight of the family home. He could also be seen, pipe in mouth, puffing away and pottering in the garden.

Prior to the birth of her four daughters (Betty, Pauline, Sheila and Geraldine), Mabel had been a regular Goodison Park attendee, but her priorities had changed to reflect her domestic commitments; nonetheless, she made a point of never missing a cup tie. Once, she intended going to a Merseyside derby, but when ten relatives turned up from Ireland for breakfast, lunch and tea on the day of the match, she had to cancel her football plans.

Eldest daughter Betty had been born in Ireland in 1952 during the close season, followed by Pauline in 1954. Pat Laverty, the daughter of a neighbour on Thirlmere Drive and not yet ten herself, had become an honorary 'nursemaid' to the Farrell children – practically becoming one of the family. A mid-1950s *Liverpool Echo* feature on the Farrell family incorporated a series of photos, one of which was of Pat and Betty stood next to a pram containing the toddler, Pauline. What the photo did not reveal was that Pauline had got stuck in the contraption and took some releasing from it. Pat's father, who was the proud owner of a car, would frequently give Peter and clubmate Don Donovan, who lived a few houses down the street, a lift to matches. The third-born daughter, Sheila, showed great ball-kicking talent as a small child, and Peter would muse that if she had been a boy she would have been playing international football by the age of 16. Both entering this world in Liverpool, Pauline and Sheila (born in 1956) would not have qualified for to play Ireland at that time, but in the modern era they could have had their pick of Ireland, England and the USA.

Being club captain extended beyond the pitch and training ground; Peter believed in seeing to the wellbeing of his clubmates. A new Irish arrival at Goodison in 1952, Mick Meagan, was briefly put up in Thirlmere Drive by the Farrells until he found his feet in the city. He would repay the kindness, with interest, as described in a later chapter. Other players joining the club would routinely be invited to Sunday dinner at Thirlmere Drive, to avoid the loneliness of being sat alone in their lodgings.

10
THE IRISH TOFFEES

As alluded to already, by the early 1950s, Peter and Tommy had been joined by no fewer than five Irishmen on the Blues' books. Fellow Dubliner Jimmy O'Neill was a young goalkeeper who would have the unenviable task of trying to dislodge the evergreen Ted Sagar from between the posts. Also from Dublin was George Cummins, a one-time hurling specialist who was given a successful trial at Goodison when over to visit his friend Jimmy O'Neill. Tommy Clinton also hailed from Ireland's capital city, but the full-back was spotted by Everton when playing for Dalgan Rovers. After initially refusing to move across the Irish Sea, he was enticed from Dundalk Rovers 18 months later. From Cork came John Sutherland and the aforementioned Don Donovan. The latter had been a hurling player with the successful Glen Rovers but was picked up by Everton after impressing as an inside-forward for Maymount Rovers. He would go on to play as a half-back and full-back in his time as a Toffeeman. The Farrells would often entertain the entire Everton Irish contingent at their house for what the *Liverpool Echo* described as 'supper and a real Irish evening'.

Everton had fielded Irish players before – notably Val Harris, Jack Kirwan, Bill Lacey and Alex Stevenson from the south, and Jack Coulter, Bobby Irvine, Jimmy

Everton's Irish cohort at the snooker table in December 1951. Watching Tommy Clinton with the cue are George Cummins, Don Donovan, John Sutherland, Tommy Eglington, Jimmy O'Neill and Peter

Sheridan and Billy Cook from the north. The son of a successful jockey, Alf Ringstead was on amateur forms with the Toffees in the war years before finding fame at Sheffield United and becoming an international teammate of Peter. Kirwan and Harris were senior All-Ireland Gaelic Football Championship winners with Dublin prior to playing for Everton. The Toffees are, to this day, the only English club to have had two All-Ireland winners play for them.

The first Everton supporters club outside of England was in Dublin, formed in the 1930s, clear confirmation of the ties between Merseyside and Ireland. This 'Irish branch' of Toffeedom gets namechecked in *Teems of Times*, the memoir of Dominic Behan, the noted Irish author, playwright, songwriter and republican. This was the start of a tradition of supporters taking the night boat to Liverpool, with most, if not all, making it to see the matches at Goodison Park before the sea passage home.

However, the club's concentration of Roman Catholic players from the south of the Emerald Isle in the 1950s was unprecedented. This gave rise to, or at the very least reinforced, the perception of the Toffees as the Roman Catholic-orientated club in the city. But was this really the case? The theory was, perhaps, lent credence by Liverpool FC not having a senior player of Irish Catholic background since County Wexford-born Bill Lacey, a former Everton star who represented the Reds either side of the First World War. Thus, it takes no great leap to consider Liverpool as the Protestant club in the city and, by extension, the Toffees as Catholic-leaning. The reality is far more nuanced.

Everton and Liverpool football clubs have shared roots in St Domingo Methodist Connexion Chapel on Breckfield Road North. Direct influence on the team from that place of worship quickly waned, as evidenced by it rebranding as Everton FC just a year after its formation. John Houlding, Everton's president and benefactor

Two of Ireland's great captains, Johnny Carey and Peter Farrell, shake hands in their club colours before a match gets underway at Goodison Park.

from the early 1880s through to 1892, was a member of the (Protestant) Orange Order as well as being a Conservative in the political realm. By contrast, following the 1892 split which led to Houlding forming Liverpool FC, the Toffees had a largely Liberal Party leaning board of directors. Dr James Baxter, who had provided a loan to ensure the construction of Goodison Park progressed, was both a Liberal councillor and a practising Roman Catholic. Dublin-born George Mahon, who served as St Domingo's organist, meanwhile, became the club's first chairman.

As a rule, Liberals were considered more open to the idea of Irish Home Rule than Conservative Unionists and were generally more disposed to being sympathetic to the many Catholics in the city. The football historian David Kennedy in his book *Merseyside's Old Firm?* argues that the stark difference in the backgrounds and beliefs of the two clubs' boardroom members would not have escaped the notice of Merseysiders when choosing which team to support. The book highlighted that a significant number of the Liverpool FC board members in its early decades were in the Freemasons. With papal decrees forbidding Roman Catholics from joining the organisation, this could be taken as a sign of the Protestant influence within the Anfield club. It does not necessarily follow that Everton was significantly different in the corridors of power. For example, the author's great-grandfather, W.J. Sawyer, Everton's secretary in 1918/19 and a club director throughout the 1920s, was a high-ranking Freemason. He was extremely unlikely to have been the only one in the Toffees' boardroom.

The second half of the 19th century had seen an exodus from Ireland, due in large part to the burden of famine and poverty borne by much of the population. Many Irish people sailed into Liverpool to start afresh; by the latter part of that century, it was estimated that a quarter of the city's residents had been born across the Irish Sea. The Orange Order had a strong presence in the city (perhaps second only to Glasgow in strength and number), so it was inevitable that the influx of Catholics would lead to some simmering tensions with working-class Protestants and the Orange Order, in particular. The riots of June 1909 were a particular flashpoint. As late as the 1970s, it could be a significant issue as to who people from the Catholic and Protestant communities mixed with – dating and marriage between people of the contrasting backgrounds could prove contentious.

Bootle, which had areas with strong Irish roots, had lost its original football club in 1893 a few years after it lost out to relative upstarts Everton FC in the race to join the newly formed Football League. A successor club, the short-lived Bootle Athletic – which was briefly managed by former Everton and Ireland star Alex Stevenson – folded in 1953. Perhaps Goodison Park's slightly closer proximity than Anfield convinced some Bootle residents to adopt the Toffees' stadium as their matchday haunt. The lower parts of the Everton district, west of Great Homer Street, towards the docks. also had a significant population with Irish heritage while upper Everton areas – closer to Anfield – were made up of a predominantly Protestant population.

There has become a collective memory of scores of priests in the crowd at Goodison Park on matchdays in the post-war era, this being cited as further evidence of Everton becoming the Catholic club. Although they were, doubtless, conspicuous, the actual headcount of men of the cloth was probably more modest than is remembered.

Accurate statistics on the religious/sectarian split of the two clubs' supporter bases in the pre-war and immediate post-war eras are lacking, making it all but impossible to draw a firm conclusion. Perhaps the crowds at Anfield and Goodison largely reflected the demographics of the port city. Peter Farrell summed it up best himself when he declared that the religion on Merseyside *was* football.

According to some former Everton players the author has interviewed (sadly, most are no longer with us), the close bond between the expat Irishmen did create something of two factions in the squad. Some non-Catholic players would be slightly bemused, at first, to see Peter and his Irish colleagues dabbing on some holy water prior to a match to bring good fortune. This was not a new phenomenon; back in 1946, prior to Peter's second match for the FAI, in Madrid, Con Martin had brought some Fatima water with him on the trip. In jest, he offered some to Billy McMillen, a Protestant, as they got changed. Entering the spirit of things, McMillen took a couple of drops. Coincidentally or not, he had an excellent game and, for years afterwards, when encountering his former teammates he would enquire after the Fatima water.

When it came to socialising, there were – as a rule – two groups: the Catholics (Irish and locally born) and the Protestant lads. Of course, there were exceptions, including Eddie Wainwright, who became a good friend of Peter and Tommy Eglington. There was no great rancour or edge to this apparent 'split in the camp', it was more a case of the different circles they mixed in. Those former players interviewed stated that, although Peter may have spent more free time with Irish brethren, as Everton captain he made the effort to assist and inspire all of his clubmates. Nonetheless, one anecdote, possibly apocryphal, recounted to the author by Everton supporter Geoff Stubbs, highlighted how sectarian issues permeated football in some cities: 'The story is that Peter Farrell got the ball on the left side of the pitch. Now, Tommy Eglington was having a stinker in that match and after he made a mess when receiving Peter's pass, someone cried out from the terracing: "For Christ's sake, Peter, pass it to a Proddy!"'

In 1953, the Blues' captain was engaged by the *Liverpool Echo* to write a weekly column. The close season was filled with his recollections of his journey in football from Dalkey to Merseyside and the international stage. The series continued with more topical musings on Everton's fortunes and football more generally. Ghost-writing was out of the question for this proud Evertonian; so, once the children were tucked up in bed each evening, he enlisted the help of Mabel. Having learned shorthand as a typist in an architect's office prior to marriage, she could take dictation and type up Peter's thoughts ready for timely submission to the newspaper. Her workload was increased when Peter also took on a column in an Irish newspaper – and then there was fan mail and countless requests for autographs to respond to. With chores done, the couple could relax. Peter was fond of watching TV while happily puffing on his pipe; Mabel, meanwhile, tuned out from the programming on the box and read a book.

Peter was thrilled to have a street named after him in the early 1960s. Located in Melling, near Kirby, Farrell Close is one of four roads in the locality paying tribute to Everton and Liverpool players. Also representing the blue half of the city was (Albert) Dunlop Drive, vying for attention with (Billy) Liddell Avenue and (John) Wheeler Drive.

11
UP FOR THE CUP, BUT DOWN IN THE DUMPS

Welcome relief from the dismal grind of the 1949/50 league campaign came via an exciting run in the FA Cup. QPR, West Ham and Tottenham Hotspur were dispatched in smart order, teeing up a quarter final at the Baseball Ground against Derby County. It was, in Peter's words, an 'epic struggle'. The catalyst for victory over the Rams was described thus by the stand-in captain:

> *Shortly after the start of the second half, an incident happened which I shall never forget. During a Derby County attack on the Everton goal, the ball was crossed from the left. Harrison and our centre-half, Ted Falder, rose in a heading duel close to our goal. Falder with his superior height seemed to have the position well in hand when Harrison, unable to meet the centre owing to his lack of inches, flicked it past Falder with his hand and into the net. I was standing about three yards away, and you can imagine my feelings when I saw the referee point to the centre of the field indicating a goal. I eventually persuaded him to consult a linesman, but he hadn't seen the infringement either, and thus we were a goal down, which I and the rest of my team-mates were convinced should never have been allowed. It was just the spur we needed and we went on to win 2–1, but what a tragedy it would have been had Derby managed to win by this goal.*

This hard-fought win paved the way for a semi-final encounter with Everton's great rivals from across Stanley Park. While the Blues had wilted after the war, the Reds had won the League in 1947 and remained the stronger of the two sides. In the weeks leading to the match, excitement grew to fever pitch; this was, after all, an era of record crowds and unprecedented interest in the game – a blessed escape from post-war austerity. The venue would be Manchester's Maine Road, the match taking place on the same afternoon as the Grand National, being run at the other end of the East Lancs Road.

The day left a lasting impression on the Blues' skipper: 'I shall never forget the scene at Maine Road that Saturday afternoon as we took the field [in] glorious sunshine. Among the 75,000 spectators there must have been over 50,000 gaily bedecked in blue and white and red and white favours as they waved their rattles and gave both teams an ovation that must have astounded the neutrals present.'

The *Daily Sports News* painted a vivid picture with words of the scenes:

> *The sun blazed down from an almost cloudless sky as the first of 500 motor coaches and 36 specials trains arrived in the city. Trains left Liverpool stations every few minutes for Manchester. At Liverpool Exchange Station there were exciting scenes as thousands of football fans, queuing for the special trains, exchanged noisy greetings and humorous badinage with the race goers in the separate queues for the trains bound for Aintree and the 'National'. Long before the start, excited spectators kept up a continuous roar of rattles, cheers and counter cheers. Their mingled blue favours for Everton and red for Liverpool, made a colourful scene.*

In the event, Liverpool had comfortably the better side, advancing to the final thanks to goals from left-back Bob Paisley and Scottish forward Billy Liddell. The former scored with a speculative lob into the box while the latter's goal came about after the linesman had failed to spot the ball going out of play. Graciously, Peter described it as a 'memorable game which was a credit to Merseyside for the sporting manner in which it was played', but privately hoped that one day it would be Everton's turn.

After the final whistle, the heartbroken Everton captain went to the Liverpool dressing room to offer his congratulations and wish the victors well in the final. A short while later, Liverpool's Phil Taylor visited the downbeat Everton dressing room to commiserate and empathise; he explained that the Reds had tasted the same bitter feeling of defeat when losing to Burnley (ironically, then managed by Cliff Britton) in a replayed semi-final in 1947.

Four days later, Everton resumed their seemingly annual battle to avoid relegation with a home fixture against West Bromwich. The Blues went down 1–0 to the Throstles but, redeployed at inside-forward, Peter gave a typically determined and inspirational display which merited comment from Leslie Edwards in the Daily Post: 'Peter Farrell has never worked harder or with more success as an individual. That

On tour with Everton in Sweden in 1950. Seated on the right is future Everton manager Harry Catterick

such unflagging effort should not have led to a least one goal was tragic.' He would wear the number ten shirt for the final matches of the league programme, with two Easter wins over Blackpool and a final day defeat of Manchester City guaranteeing safety for another year. However, having played Russian roulette with relegation for several seasons, there was an inevitability to the Toffees' supply of luck being exhausted, in spite of Peter's boundless enthusiasm and inspirational leadership.

Restored to the left-half position, and formally re-appointed club captain in the wake of T.G. Jones' departure for life as a player-manager and hotelier in Pwllheli, the Dalkey man was ever-present for Everton in the 1950/51 season. Jackie Grant, a diminutive but brave and pugnacious north-easterner who had joined the Toffees during the war years, filled the other wing-half spot. This was a poor Everton side. Signings were few and far between as the hierarchy focused on youth development. When the club did spend big, it appeared to be ill-judged and lacking the calibre to turn around its ailing fortunes. Aubrey Powell underwhelmed after being signed for a club record £10,000 fee from Leeds United in 1948. Harry Potts was just six days shy of his 30th birthday, and probably on the decline, when signing from Burnley for another record fee of £20,000 in October 1950. Infamously, Albert Juliussen arrived injured from Portsmouth shortly before Cliff Britton became manager in 1948 and never recovered form or fitness; the Toffees even fruitlessly sought some recompense from the Hampshire team.

In spite of their poor track record in the transfer market, safety for another year seemed to be well within grasp with two wins in late February putting the Blues in 15th place. A badly broken leg had robbed the side of the services of the quicksilver and in-form forward Eddie Wainwright, while the industrious Cyril Lello was absent all season with knee problems. Without their contributions, the goals dried up and only one further victory would come in the final 12 fixtures of the season. That win, in the penultimate match, appeared to have staved off the seemingly inexorable slide into the relegation places. A draw away to already relegated Sheffield Wednesday on the last day of the season would see the Blues dodge the bullet once more.

In preparation, the squad decamped again to Buxton, staying in the same hotel as Everton's side just prior to the 1933 FA Cup final. On the Saturday morning, the party boarded the coach for the trip across the Peak District to the Steel City. Thousands of messages of good luck by card and telegram were received, including one from Liverpool FC.

Ted Sagar had been unable to overcome a thigh injury, so George Burnett was entrusted with the goalkeeper duties. Future Blues manager Harry Catterick led the offensive line. Prior to kick-off, the Toffees were inundated with telegrams wishing the side good luck, including one from Liverpool FC.. Peter won the toss but it had little advantage in conditions described by Don Kendall, writing as Pilot in the *Evening Express*, as 'dismal for there was a cross-field wind taking with it a slow penetrating drizzle'. After 15 minutes of dominance at Hillsborough, the away side endured a number of calamitous defensive moments and conceded three goals in eight first-half minutes, beginning with a slip by T.E. Jones on 23 minutes which let Woodhead in on goal. The Owls scored a fourth and had a penalty brilliant saved by Burnett early in the second half, but news filtered through of Chelsea leading against Bolton, meaning that both sides at Hillsborough faced the drop. Two further goals by the home side consigned the Toffees to a humiliating 6–0 defeat and relegation. After a bright start, the Everton performance had few positives, Pilot described Tommy Eglington as the only forward to demonstrate any consistency, while of Peter he wrote: 'Peter Farrell, the inimitable, ran himself into the ground to try to stave off what even his big heart must have known.'

When penning his life story a few years later, the captain reflected on this low point of his career and the remarkable support received from some Everton supporters in the face of adversity:

> I wish you could have seen the faces of the Everton lads in the dressing room after this game against Sheffield Wednesday. You would think each one of them had lost a very dear relative. Here I must pay tribute to our manager, Mr. Cliff Britton, who came in and did his best to cheer the lads up despite the fact that he was probably feeling the disappointment more than anyone. Sometime later when the many thousands of people had left the ground and were homeward bound, we came out to board our

coach feeling as I have already mentioned a very dejected lot.

Outside the ground, alongside our coach was a small band of Evertonians, who gave us a reception we never deserved. As the coach pulled away, I shall never forget that loyal little following whom we had let down so badly, as, waving their scarves and rattles, they shouted, 'Don't worry lads, we will be back again soon.' They are all fairly well known to the lads and myself as we see them outside practically every away ground, yes, some of them were even outside Upton Park last year. They are the best supporters any club could wish to have, and we are very proud of them.

Unsurprisingly, many Toffees fanatics were less forgiving of this new nadir in the club's fortunes. Musing on how the club had sunk this low, Bob Prole, writing as 'Ranger' in the *Liverpool Echo*, was concise but brutal in his assessment: 'The need is for players of outstanding ability in the key positions and Everton haven't had them since the departure of Mercer, Lawton, Stevenson and T.G. Jones. With the possible exception of Farrell there isn't a player who stands out like any of the old pre-war championship side. The team too long has lacked personality. The players that have been brought, Potts apart, have all been more or less mediocre performers. Earnest triers – good for a bright performance now and again, but no more.'

Eight days after Everton's catastrophic result at Hillsborough, Peter was lining up for Ireland, earning his first international cap in 18 months. The opponents were Argentina, who became the first South American opponents to grace Dalymount. Their incentive to make the transatlantic journey was a guarantee of £1,500 or half of the gate money, whichever was greater. The all-ticket affair (a first at Dalymount) attracted a 40,000 crowd which saw a narrow 1-0 defeat for the hosts. Three weeks later, Peter's domestic close season was further eaten into when he was called up for the Ireland fixture in Oslo. He scored one of the two Irish equalising goals against the Norwegian side before Paddy Coad netted the winner. The trip was otherwise notable for the FAI being inspired by the Norwegian FA's practice of awarding a gold watch to players reaching the 25 international appearance milestone. It was moved to introduce a silver shamrock on a base of Connemara polished marble, weighing 28lb (12.7kg), to mark present to Irish players reaching the quarter century. Johnny Carey who was making his 27th appearance for the FAI's national side, in Norway, would become the first recipient of the striking ornament.

12
THE RELEGATION HANGOVER

The bitterness of relegation had only been tasted once previously, in 1930, and the club's AGM of 1951, held in June, was a stormy affair. Shareholders didn't hold back in conveying their anger and long-serving director Dick Searle was voted off the board. Ironically, it fell to an Arsenal player among the attendees to appeal for calm and togetherness. Five years after switching from Goodison Park to Highbury, Joe Mercer still held an Everton share, so was present as a voice of reason, pleading for unity in the club's darkest hour.

Relegation notwithstanding, manager Cliff Britton retained the backing of the board and remained in post. He had no hesitation in asking Peter to continue as captain as the Blues prepared for life in the second tier of the Football League. The financial hit of relegation from the top flight was far less than it is now in the Premier League era – that, combined with the wage cap, the absence of freedom of contract for players, and a continued focus on developing homegrown talent, meant that the squad was largely unchanged.

Britton experimented with putting Peter back to inside-left (at the expense of Wally Fielding), to partner his great friend 'Eggo' on the left flank – with Cyril Lello coming in as wing-half behind them. Ranger (*Liverpool Echo*) commented: 'Farrell figured in the forwards two seasons ago on 18 occasions at both inside right and inside left. After getting a goal in each of his first two games, however, he lost the pattern and did not score again. But Farrell is a grand worker, and if honest effort and club spirit can do the trick, he will not be found wanting.' After a disappointing opening-day defeat to Southampton (in which Harry Potts and Peter were described as working like Trojans) the experiment was rapidly abandoned, and the popular leader spent the majority of games in his customary number six shirt.

Whereas the Toffees had bounced straight back from relegation in 1930 with promotion at the first attempt, there was to be no fairytale return in 1951/52. Harry Catterick would cede his centre-forward spot to a young Dave Hickson a few matches into the season. Hickson, who became idolised for his fearless approach on the pitch, said this of his captain in the late 1990s: 'Peter had the same attitude to football as myself. He gave 110 per cent every match and you couldn't help but play for the man. He was where my inspiration came from: him and Cliff Britton, the manager. He was an incredibly dedicated footballer; he was devastated when he was captain of the side which was relegated. He wouldn't give up on any ball and was a great man to have on your side. I suppose if you were to compare him to a modern-day footballer you would choose somebody like Joe Parkinson.'

Even the impact of the so-called Cannonball Kid was not enough to push the Blues into the reckoning for a return to the First Division. A seventh-place position, seven points off the promotion places, was a modest return — in contrast to fellow demoted side, Sheffield Wednesday, who were crowned champions.

The season, in which Everton recorded a gross profit of £8,655, ended with the side's young goalkeeper Jimmy O'Neill joining Peter and Tommy Eglington in the Ireland squad to face Spain in Madrid on 1 June. Another Everton Irishman, Tommy Clinton, was chosen as the reserve. O'Neill had a baptism of fire, conceding six goals with Ireland unable to

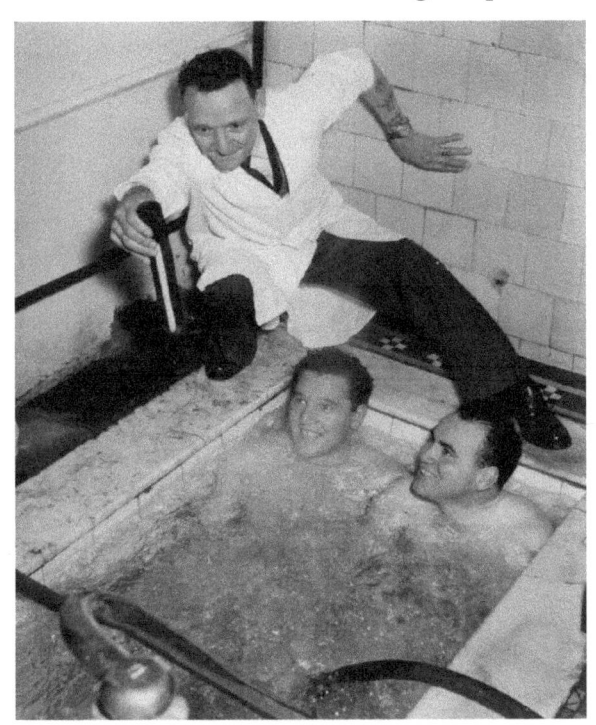

The skipper enjoying the curative effect of the waters in Buxton alongside Everton goalkeeper Harry Leyland

threaten the Spanish net. On a happier note, the previous October, in the absence of the aging Johnny Carey, Peter had captained Ireland to a midweek 3–2 victory over West Germany at Dalymount. Eglington had a particularly fine game, tormenting the German rearguard and setting new cap Dessie Glynn up for the winner.

Looking back on the season, Ranger (in the *Football Echo*) felt that the captain's enthusiasm and unrelenting effort were sometimes to his detriment: 'As much as I admire Peter Farrell, he is still a little inclined to do the work himself rather than let the ball do it for him. There is no harder or more loyal player than the Irish International and his example is always an inspiration, but if he could conserve his energies somewhat and use the ball to greater advantage, instead of trying to take it up too far himself, I think it would be a helpful factor.'

Hopes that Everton might push for promotion in 1952/53, after a period of acclimatisation to the Second Division, proved ill-founded. An abysmal 16th-place finish (with 22 sides in the division) was only partially offset by progress in the FA Cup. The fifth-round home tie against Matt Busby's Manchester United on Valentine's Day 1953 has attained mythical status for Dave Hickson's heroics. Having sustained gashes from a boot to the head when flinging himself at a cross, the talismanic centre-forward went off for stitches, returning to the fray shortly after the interval, but still dabbing the wound with a handkerchief. In the process of crashing

Everton training, 1950s-style. Peter, wearing what looks like pinstripe trousers, follows Harry Leyland as the lads get in some running practice near the East Lancs Road

the ball against a post, he opened up the wound again and the blood flowed. As skipper, Peter was informed by referee Mr Beacock, 'He'll have to go off. He can't go on with an eye like that. He's not normal.' The Cannonball Kid, overhearing the conversation, interjected: 'I heard that, ref, I am normal. Tell him I'm normal, Peter, tell him!'

Playing the fatherly captain role, Peter turned to his bloodied centre-forward and replied, 'Of course you are, Dave.' Hearing the soothing words, Hickson shouted, 'There you are, ref! I'm staying!' Mr Beacock thought better than to prolong the

Dressing room celebrations after a cup win in 1953. Manager Cliff Britton, sometimes considered somewhat aloof, was a huge admirer of his captain.

debate, and acquiesced. The script was then written for the striker to steal the show. With 63 minutes on the clock, he collected a ball from Tommy Eglington and hit an unstoppable drive past Wood in the United net. It sealed a thrilling 2–1 victory, the Toffees coming back from a goal down.

The blond, luxuriantly quiffed number nine was on the mark again when scoring the decisive goal in the quarter-final tie at Aston Villa. His goal close to the hour mark, the only one of the match, triggered a wave of delirium in the massed ranks of the Blues travelling support at Villa Park. One attendee, Louis Hickey, told his son Francis that there were so many vociferous Evertonians in the ground that the Villa players put their hands to their ears when Everton came onto the pitch prior to kick-off. It reputedly prompted the first written reference to the 'Goodison Roar', even though it

In the thick of it, where Peter liked to be

was at an away fixture. This display of passion presages similar scenes at the same stadium in 1984, when the Toffees advanced to the League Cup final, the two FA Cup semi-final wins in 1985 and 1986, and following Kevin Sheedy's volley in front of a massive away following at Easter 1987, as the team advanced on the league title.

Victory over Villa meant that the Blues advanced to a semi-final against Bolton Wanderers, to be staged at Maine Road, Manchester. Here was an opportunity to atone for going down 2–0 to Liverpool at the same stage of the competition in 1950. 'As we took to the field, I had a feeling of confidence mingled with hope that this was going to be our year,' said Peter. However, such thoughts were quickly extinguished as a strangely subdued Everton were blown away by their opponents.

With nine minutes gone Holden had put Wanderers in the lead – and it got worse, much worse. As half-time approached, the ragged Toffees outfit trailed 4–0. Jimmy O'Neill would normally have expected to save two, perhaps three of the efforts but had a nervy half. The superstitious might have put his dip in form down to him forgetting the small silver-cardboard horseshoe with a black cat attached, sent to him in January by his little niece in Ireland. He had brought it with him to the previous cup fixtures but had left it behind in error at home. He asked his brother, over from Ireland, to collect it and drop it off at the Maine Road changing rooms but, alas, he left it behind in the car which had taken him to Manchester. The goalkeeper was said to be very upset about the absence of his lucky charm. To add to the woes, Dave Hickson had taken a heavy blow to the face and been off the field for a quarter of an hour, returning to see out the match in a state of concussion.

Then, with two minutes to the interval, a lifeline was given to Blues through a spot kick, which Tommy Clinton stepped forward to take. Lacking both power and placement, his effort went tamely past the post.

Peter, who subsequently wondered if the players had been too keyed up for the match, recalled that they were very disappointed in themselves as they trudged towards the changing rooms at half-time where the manager was waiting to rally them: 'A few encouraging words from our manager, Mr Britton, cheered us up considerably and we came out for the second half to the sound of a tumultuous ovation from our supporters, which couldn't have been bettered had we had been leading 4–0.'

John Willie Parker's glancing header from a Buckle corner had restored some pride, but Bolton went into the final minutes leading 4–1. Then a twice-taken free-kick ended with Peter's 20-yard drive finding its way through a crowded penalty area and into the net. Parker nodded the ball over the line with six minutes left to bring the Blues within a goal of the Trotters. The disbelieving Evertonians, estimated at 30,000, found their voice but, despite peppering the Bolton goal with shots, the Blues could not add an equaliser.

Looking back, the captain mused, 'Although we were very disappointed that our rally had just failed to come off, we were pleased that we had at least gone out fighting.'

The end of the season brought to a close the remarkable playing career of Ted Sagar. The Yorkshire-born goalkeeper had been with the Toffees for 24 years, racking up a then club record 497 appearances before ceding his place in the side to Harry Leyland and Jimmy O'Neill. He bowed out at Goodison in the Liverpool Senior Cup final – a 4-1 defeat of Tranmere Rovers. At the final whistle, to huge cheers he was chaired off the pitch by Peter and Tommy E. Jones. However, he would don his football boots one last time on 20 June in the unlikely setting of Westport, County Mayo, to mark the opening of the coastal town's sports centre. Peter oversaw and captained a strong Everton XI while Sagar kept goal in a Johnny Carey XI which also included Con Martin and Wally Fielding in the lineup. Not only was it a swansong for Sagar; Carey was making his final appearance. In incessant rain, the veteran pair could not prevent Tommy Eglington, Dave Hickson and Cyril Lello from scoring in a 3-1 win for the Toffees.

13
REDEMPTION

There was more stability to the 1953/54 season – nine players made 30 or more league appearances – with a rejuvenated Cyril Lello and Don Donovan ever-present on 42. The Hickson–Parker attacking partnership would register 55 goals (31 to Parker, the superb sniffer of chances) while Eddie Wainwright was also back in the side, and the goals, after two years out with a badly broken leg. Wainwright, although of a quiet disposition, was well-liked and struck up friendships with several teammates, including Peter and Tommy Eglington. The forward had a meagre appetite in the build-up to matches, so the Irish duo would sit either side of him at lunch and whisper in his ear, 'Eddie, order the steak'. They'd then polish it off for him. Wainwright would also play golf every Monday with his steak-devouring pals plus Don Donovan. Eglington would reminisce after Eddie's passing: 'Eddie was always a great teammate. He was a very helpful man in every way possible and, of course, he was also a very good footballer.'

A solid start saw the side unbeaten until early October, with the skipper sensing

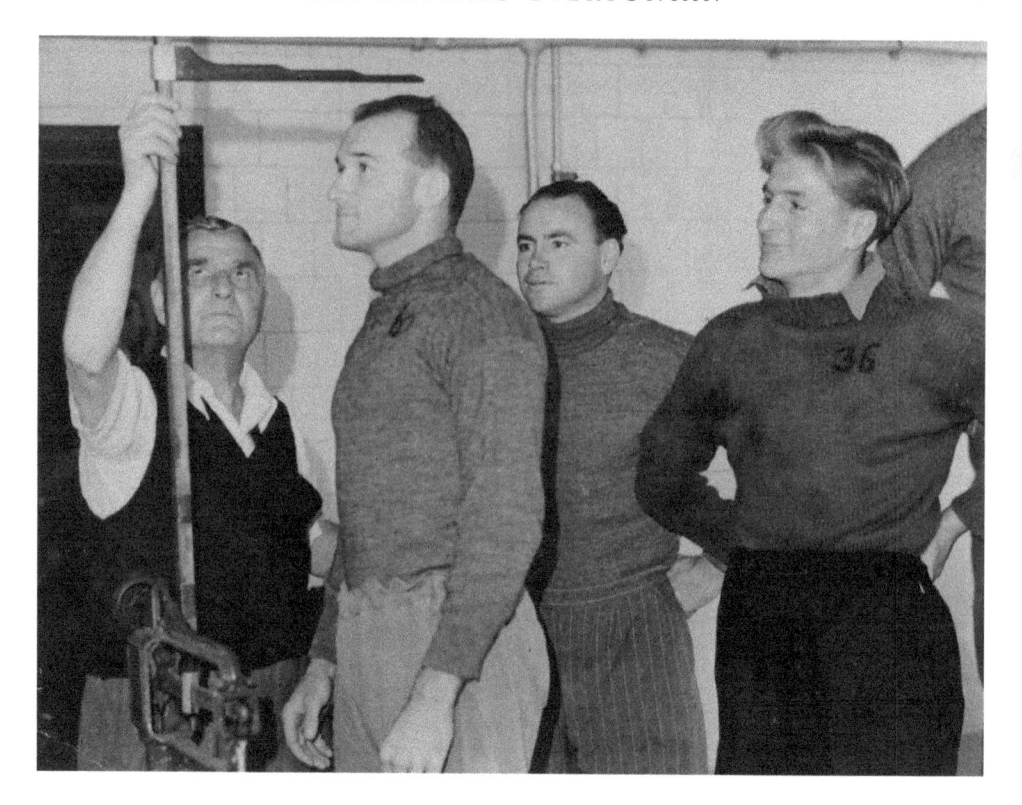

Gordon 'Gogie' Stewart, who had arrived from Vancouver in 1953 to spend a year with Everton, gets measured by the legendary Blues' trainer, Harry Cooke. Peter and Dave Hickson are there to welcome the Canadian to Goodison Park.

that this would be their season: 'I was confident we were going to be in the running for promotion by the time April came around. The pessimists shook their hands and said, "Wait and see."'

The mid-season spell, from 12 December to 20 March inclusive, saw Everton go 13 games without defeat. Six goals were put past Derby County and Brentford, and eight past Plymouth. As fatigue and, perhaps, nerves took their toll, there were consecutive defeats, at home to West Ham on Grand National Day and away to Leeds United. This dropped Everton from first to third place in the league, with just two promotion spots up for grabs, with Leicester, Blackburn Rovers, Birmingham City and Nottingham Forest also in the mix.

These defeats were followed by a home draw with Stoke. The Potters took the lead in 17 minutes and just three minutes later John Lindsay suffered a compound fracture of his leg in preventing the visitors from doubling their lead. Lindsay would never recover to the level required to play for Everton again (coincidentally, on the same afternoon, Joe Mercer sustained a fractured leg when playing for Arsenal against Liverpool, bringing down the curtain on his remarkable playing career, which had briefly overlapped with Peter at Goodison Park).

The Blues showed the grit all good sides require in times of adversity, playing for

70 minutes with ten men and grabbing an equaliser through Dave Hickson with 13 minutes to go. Normal service was resumed at home to Lincoln City with, unusually, Peter getting in on the scoring act in a 3–1 win.

Two away draws and a narrow home victory over Birmingham City meant that victory at Oldham Athletic on the final day of the Blues season would guarantee promotion. A six-goal winning margin would confirm the Toffees as champions, just ahead of Leicester City on goal average (goal difference was introduced in 1976)

The original fixture at Boundary Park had been abandoned due to fog, so this

A dressing room scene. Note the branded Everton towels, the poor state of the socks and the lightweight training shoes

immensely important match was rescheduled to a Thursday evening (6:50pm), 29 April, with the Everton side cognisant of what was required. Success-starved Evertonians headed in droves for the Lancashire mill town, either on the three chartered trains or along the East Lancs Road in more than 100 motor coaches. Many found themselves locked out, some resorting to clambering over the stadium walls, which were coated with tar to deter such actions. Undeterred, enterprising ascenders put newspapers onto the tar to protect their clothing. Those less daring or agile had to follow events on the pitch from the street or nearby hostelries. The situation was so chaotic outside the packed ground that three or four of the players' girlfriends, who had complimentary tickets, were unable to gain admission and saw none of the match action.

The Latics' goalkeeper was the former Everton glovesman George Burnett. Still a Toffee at heart, he was reportedly less than devastated when the visitors put four first-half goals past him. Everton could not add the two goals to the tally required to finish the season as champions, but it mattered not. Promotion had been achieved at the third attempt; Everton were back in the big time.

When the whistle blew to end the match, jubilant Blues flooded the pitch and mobbed the players. For Peter, the enormity of what had been achieved after three years of hurt hit him in those moments of euphoria: 'It is very hard to describe my feelings and those of the other Everton players ... As I was chaired off the field I was nearly overcome with emotion.' The supporters then refused to leave the pitch, chanting 'We want Peter!' until the captain had come to the front of the stand and taken a bow. His voice breaking, he proudly told the Evertonians present that he had been skipper when the team was relegated, and now he had captained the side back up to the First Division. He later recalled: 'As I watched the vast sea of happy people, disappointed so often, I knew they had, at last, been rewarded for their loyalty.'

The atmosphere in the dressing room was one of ecstasy. Players embraced and the usually stiff-lipped Cliff Britton was, in Peter's opinion, the happiest he had ever been.

> *It was certainty the greatest moment of my life and I know from the look of the lads in the bath after the game that they were experiencing the same emotion. You can imagine the feeling of our team when we all realised that, at last, we had given our supporters some reward for the way they have stood by us through thick and thin. The fact that Everton are now back where they belong in Division One can be attributed in no small way to the team spirit of the boys that made it possible. Whatever our faults and irrespective of whether we played well or badly, one thing predominated over everything else, namely that to every game during the season we were all pals both on and off the field.*

In a show of great sportsmanship, Johnny Carey came into the changing room to congratulate Britton and his players, in spite of his Blackburn Rovers side being pipped for promotion by a point. He told Britton that it was only right that Everton should be in the top level of the English game.

Back in Liverpool, those that could not make it to the game waited excitedly for special editions of the evening newspaper to be published. The switchboard of the *Daily Post* was jammed with enquiries about the score. The match result was announced in the city's cinemas, while local hostelries reported doing excellent business.

On the final few miles of the journey back along the East Lancs Road, Evertonians turned out in force to cheer the coach, and on arrival back at Goodison Park, around midnight, Peter and his teammates – exhausted but elated – had their backs slapped by enthusiastic supporters. After a quick toast of orangeade to the skipper, they headed home for a well-deserved rest.

Everton chairman Ernest Green's praise was succinct but warm: 'All the players have done well, but a special word of praise is due to Peter Farrell, who had the added responsibility of captaincy in a season full of tension. He has fulfilled those duties both on and off the field, by a most creditable manner. As far as my recollection goes the club has had no better captain.'

When asked to name the night's outstanding player, Cliff Britton had little hesitation: 'They all played well, but Peter Farrell kept us up to scratch right through the season – and he didn't let us down tonight.' Peter, for his part, was having none of it: 'I attribute our success to our work as a team. With sportsmen such as ours, we have no need of a captain.'

A few days later, Peter used his *Echo* column to acknowledge the fanatical support of the side:

> *On behalf of the rest of the team and myself, I should like to say how grateful we all are for the numerous telegrams and letters which we have received congratulating us on gaining promotion. One of the most touching letters received by myself was from a young girl of 10 years, who wrote 'Dear Mr. Farrell thank you very much for making my daddy so happy.' One of the first into the dressing room at Oldham after the game was my old friend Jackie Carey whose team we just pipped on the post.*

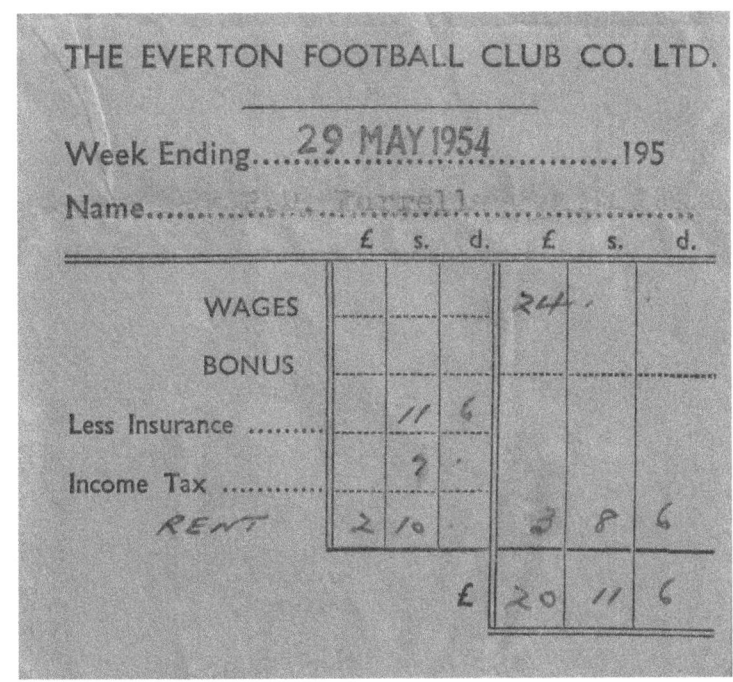

Peter's wage packet for the week ending 29 May 1954. He would take home £20 after deductions for insurance, tax and the rent on his club house.

Jackie's remark to me was typical of the sportsman and gentleman we all know him to be. 'I'm glad, Peter,' he said 'not only for your sake, but for the sake of football, as there is only one place for a team with the ground, support and tradition of Everton and that is the First Division.'

Promotion was made all the sweeter by the news that the Blues would be swapping places with Liverpool, the Reds having been relegated to the Second Division. The Anfield club's manager Don Welsh was magnanimous when he learned of the Toffees' result at Oldham: 'That's good news. I congratulate Everton, and hope that we'll meet the season after next.'

As it panned out, it would be eight years before they met again in the top flight, but the great rivals did get to meet in the Liverpool Senior Cup final to round off the 1953/54 season. Both clubs fielded their strongest sides at Goodison Park on 3 May, with bragging rights at stake. Stork, writing for the *Liverpool Daily Post*, noted, 'In the first half Everton touched really top form. They ran into the open spaces, switched about, in fact, they did everything a good footballing team should do.' Although the Toffees let the Reds back into the match in the second half, John Willie Parker, the ace goal-poacher, gave the home side the lead after being set up by Dave Hickson. The Cannonball Kid wrapped up the scoring in the final minutes when, fed by Wally Fielding, he put a fizzer past the watching Underwood in the Liverpool goal. The popularity of football in the post-war years is illustrated by the 52,012 gate for the final of what is considered a secondary competition.

One day after the culmination of the domestic season, Everton were honoured in the candle-lit dining room of Liverpool Town Hall. Lord Mayor Alderman W.J. Tristram hosted the dinner and, speaking on behalf of the citizens of Liverpool, declared, 'It has been a hard road and a very trying time for directors, officials and players but you are back where you belong.' Alderman J.J. Cleary added, 'Football has a great place in the life of Liverpool, and I hope that our two great teams will go from fame to fame and add to the lustre of this city.'

14
THE QUEST TO QUALIFY FOR THE WORLD CUP FINALS

Peter had remained a mainstay of the Irish national team – albeit with relatively few fixtures organised each year, except when World Cup qualification was underway. The qualifiers for the 1954 World Cup finals saw Ireland drawn against France and Luxembourg. These were proceeded by a friendly against Austria at Dalymount for which a record five players were called up from Everton: Jimmy O'Neill, Peter, Tommy Eglington, Tommy Clinton and new selectee George Cummins. In the event Clinton had to withdraw, and Cummins could not play due to a suspension at club level.

Relations between the FAI and the Toffees were enhanced by the appointment of Alex Stevenson as the trainer-coach of the national side. The Dubliner, who had enjoyed 15 years at Goodison Park, would have used his close connections and natural charm to get the co-operation of the Everton directors. By contrast, many English clubs were minded to decline FAI requests to release their players. In fairness, they had some justification for this lack of co-operation. At full-time their star players would have to dash from their club matches, with their boots hastily cleaned of mud, and make for the nearest port with a ferry link to Rosslare, to Dublin or nearby Dún Laoghaire. These night sailings would berth on the Irish side of the sea sometime after breakfast. Dún Laoghaire football historian Joe Dodd recalls a friend from that era who lived next to the harbour, and would watch the footballers disembarking, then walking up Marine Road to get the bus up to Dublin. Peter would have been a local hero to those watching this scene, having been raised just a few miles away.

From landfall, the players had precious little time to reach the Gresham Hotel for a light bite and a team talk prior to proceeding to Dalymount Park in the city's northern suburbs for the match. Then, on full-time, the rigmarole would be repeated, but in reverse – a dash to the ferry terminal, an overnight crossing to England and then an onwards journey by road or rail to home, ready for club training on the Monday.

In these qualifiers, Ireland once again struggled with some players not being released – notably Alf Ringstead of Sheffield United. With the retirement of Johnny Carey (who had accepted the position of manager of Blackburn Rovers), Peter was, on his 21st international FAI appearance, named captain for the visit of the French team to Dalymount in October 1953. When sounded out about the team's chances in what was being billed as one of the most important matches in Irish football history, the pipe-puffing skipper was bullish: 'I think we have a good chance of victory. We are all fit, in top form and should give a good display. We know one weakness of the French team – they do not like hard tackling.' He was asked to comment on the 'funnel' system of defence deployed in the previous match and responded that he was very much in favour: 'With a bank of defenders in the penalty area, every yard they advance and every yard we retreat lessens their chance of scoring.' Alex Stevenson, meanwhile, declared his players to be 'as fit as fiddles', but was hoping for a spot of rain to make the pitch conditions heavier, to suit the Irish game plan.

After training the day before the match, both teams attended a reception hosted by the Lord Mayor, followed by a cocktail party at the French Legion and a night out at the Theatre Royal.

Special supporters' trains were laid on from Belfast, Sligo, Galway, Cork, Limerick and Waterford, helping to swell the crowd to over 44,000. The perceptive W.P. Murphy (*Irish Independent*) highlighted the need to get through the first ten minutes without conceding, to provide a platform for Irish success and help generate the 'Dalymount Roar'. The plan appeared to be working but then Léon Glovacki flashed a shot past Jimmy O'Neill on 22 minutes. With Joseph Ujlaki and Raymond Kopa pulling the strings for the French, a second goal was added in the opening 40 minutes and three more were put past O'Neill after the break. That said, according to W.P. Murphy, Peter and Frank O'Farrell couldn't be faulted – 'They kept a constant supply of passes to an attack that, with the exception of Ryan and Eglington, could do little with them.' Eglington was also having a fine match, running at terrific speed down the left wing and delivering crosses that, sadly, no one was able to convert.

Trailing 5–1 with 15 minutes left on the clock, the home side made a surprising late surge. Davy Walsh tapped home a low centre and then, as the final whistle approached, Peter received a ball from Eglington and teed up O'Farrell for a superb first-time shot. Pride may have been restored, but the Irish were left with the nigh-on-impossible task of beating France in the return match, six weeks later, to keep their World Cup hopes alive. Before that came the qualifying match against Luxembourg (a 4–0 victory), for which Peter was controversially overlooked, as the selectors tried some younger options.

The selectors reverted to experience for the match in Paris. The trip so nearly ended in tragedy as the aircraft flying the England-based Irish players to France came within feet of disaster, as Peter recalled in his *Echo* column:

> *I have a vivid recollection of our flight from London. It was a very foggy night as our aircraft circled over the airport preparatory to landing. Visibility was very poor as we started to land, and I received a terrible fright when we were about 30 feet from the ground. The plane gave a sudden jerk and immediately started to ascend again before proceeding to another airport about 15 minutes away where we landed safely. I still shudder at the thought of what might have happened had the pilot not noticed in time, through the fog, that he was about to land not on the runway but on rough ground bordering it.*

Safely back on *terra firma*, Everton's Tommy Clinton came into the Irish side at right-back for only his second cap. Peter would be at wing-half, in harness with Tommy Eglington on the left flank. Although France was patently the superior team, the doughty Irishmen held firm. Frank Johnstone, reporting on the match, noted: 'Farrell made many an aspiring sortie, and played with unflagging enthusiasm, to have one of his best games.' Another match report described his performance as, simply, 'brilliant'. Alas, 17 minutes from the end, by which point the hobbling Peter was little more than a passenger, a mix-up in the visitors' defence gifted possession to left-winger Léon Deladerrière, who slipped the ball inside for Piantoni to deliver the coup de grâce with a shot which almost tore the netting from its supports. And that was how the match ended – and with it, any chance of Irish participation in the finals to be held in Switzerland the following summer.

Peter and his Everton comrades were not selected for the second match against the Luxembourgers as it was a dead rubber, presenting an opportunity to further blood some new talent. Peter would have to wait 12 months to pull on the green jersey again.

Alex Stevenson would step down from his FAI role within months of accepting it, taking the player-manager position at St Patrick's Athletic. He had found his time as coach of the national team immensely frustrating due to the paucity of time spent with the squad, which made detailed tactical discussions or training sessions an impossibility, and his lack of say on squad selection (which rested firmly with the FAI committee).

15
BACK IN THE BIG TIME

When the Everton squad and officials reconvened after their 1954 summer break, along with their partners they were treated to a promotion celebration dinner at Blackpool's Imperial Hotel. The invites stipulated assembly at Goodison Park at 8:45am for a departure 15 minutes later by chartered coaches. The long day would take in a coffee stop at Hodder Bridge, near Clitheroe, prior to arrival in the seaside town in time for a 1pm cold buffet lunch at the Imperial. The afternoon was given over to taking in Blackpool's myriad attractions before sitting for dinner at 6:45pm, to a musical accompaniment of the house orchestra. The long day would conclude with drop-off back in Liverpool at 10:15pm.

The Toffees manager and directors did not see fit to reinforce the playing squad in preparation for the return of top-flight football to Goodison Park. This cautious approach appeared to be justified when the team flew out of the blocks, winning four of their first five matches in the league. A 5–2 win on the road at Sheffield United was followed by home victories over Arsenal and Preston North End. John Willie

THE EMERALD EVERTONIAN

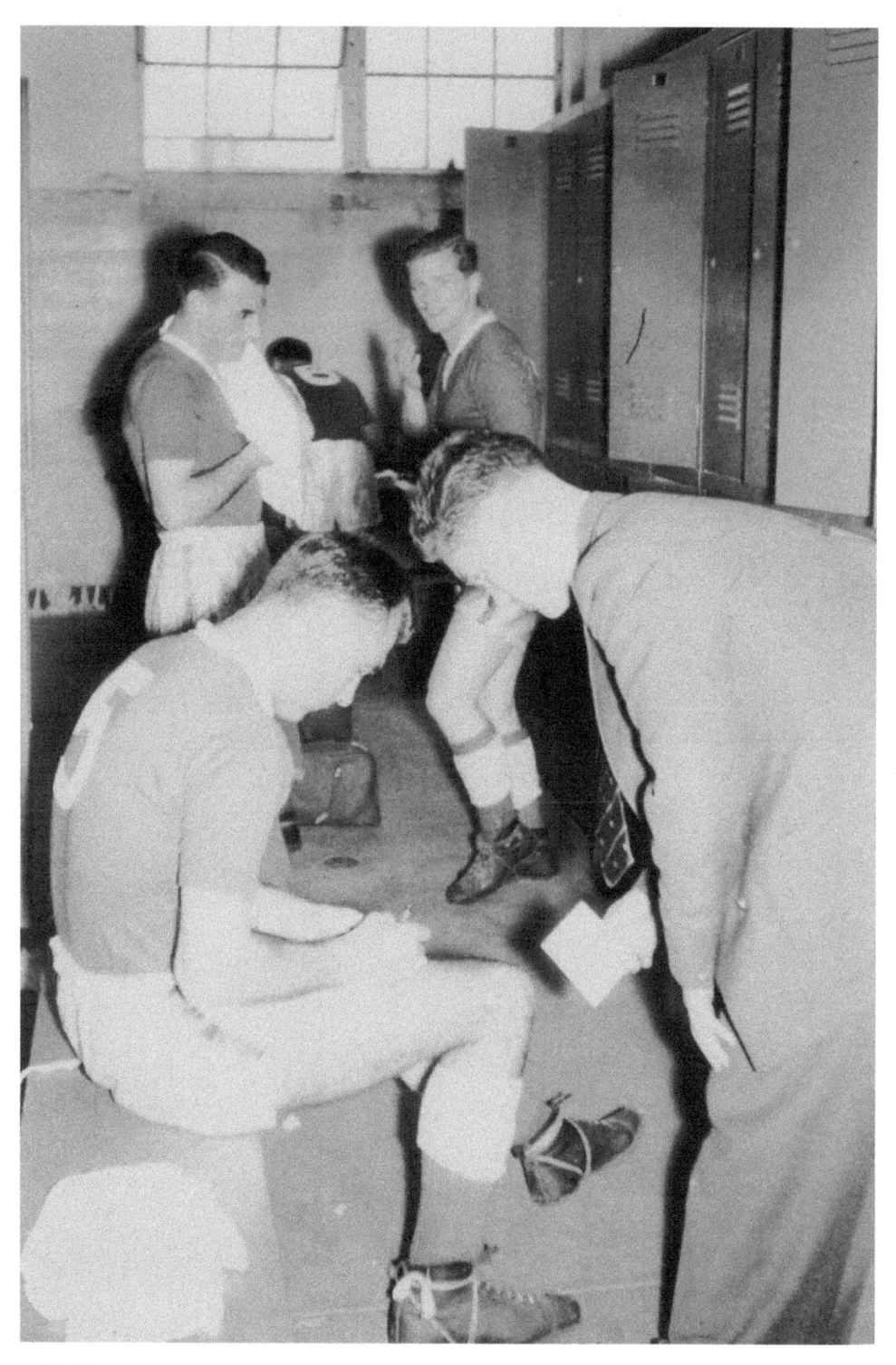

The Everton dressing room in the mid-1950s, Peter can be seen in the back of shot, wearing the number six shirt

The Everton Toffee Lady mascot offers encouragement to Peter and Jimmy O'Neill as they emerge from the players' tunnel at Villa Park. This image, probably taken in October 1954, inspired a subsequent Charles Buchan Football Monthly cover illustration.

Parker, a cunning foil to Dave Hickson with a knack for snaffling out chances, bagged 19 goals during the season, whereas the Cannonball Kid found the jump in standards more of a challenge, hitting a modest 12 in the league. With Cyril Lello, a year older than Peter, defying his age to be an ever-present at left-half, the Irishman was the pick at right-half, missing just one match, due to international commitments.

The FAI had finally insisted that British clubs release their players in good time for the Sunday matches played at Dalymount. The Irish selectors let it be known that players should be made available to report for training in Dublin on the Thursday prior to the match. With few exceptions, clubs co-operated, but the Toffees often went over and above. In November 1954, Everon's decision to omit four Irishmen (Jimmy O'Neill, Peter Farrell, Don Donovan and Tommy Eglington) from their Saturday afternoon fixture against Portsmouth led to a complaint from the Football League of them weakening their side unduly. The authorities may have had a point, although Pompey would not have been complaining as the Merseysiders crashed to a 5–0 defeat. Benefitting from a few days of rest, the Blues quartet, captained by Peter, enjoyed a 2–1 victory over Norway in Dublin, with the debutant Donovan impressing.

On the Saturday afternoon before the match, while Peter took a bus to visit friends in Dublin, a member of the Dublin Branch of the Everton Supporters Federation shouted across to inform him that the Toffees were 4–0 down at half-time at Fratton Park (Pompey ran out 5–0 winners – emphasising how much the release of a large chunk of the first-choice XI had hurt the side). Speaking at the banquet after the international match, Oscar Traynor, president of the FAI, thanked the English clubs for releasing the players for the international, but saved special praise for the Toffees: 'It was one of the greatest acts of self-sacrifice I have known in football,' he said. 'The Everton club has earned the respect and esteem of sportsmen throughout Ireland for their action, I hope they will be rewarded by figuring in the season's honours list.'

Although short on the quality required to be genuine title challengers and thereby emulate the Blues side of 1931/32 who won the top prize immediately after securing promotion, the Everton side was as high as third place in the table in late March, before sliding to 11th by losing four of the final six fixtures of the campaign. Peter, in his newspaper column, summed it up thus: 'It was a season which opened in great style but finished very disappointingly. The biggest disappointment to all of us has been the number of games in which we have held the upper hand and yet lost through not accepting our chances or through conceding goals which should not have been.'

Ranger, in his summing-up of the season in his *Echo* column, praised the evergreen wing-halves: 'Farrell and Lello too have worn amazingly well considering that they are now getting towards the veteran stage. Lello's recovery from the serious knee injury which threatened to end his career three seasons back has been excellent.'

Watching the senior pros at a respectful distance was Derek Temple, a centre-

Two posed shots at Goodison Park: Leaping and dribbling for the cameraman

forward who had joined the club's ground staff straight from school in the summer of 1954, before turning professional on reaching 17. Although consigned largely to maintenance duties and matches in the junior ranks, he would come across Peter and the senior pros around Goodison Park: 'I never played with Peter, but he was a very nice man. I remember him smoking his pipe and he looked very comfortable in that – he was the senior man. I remember sitting in the Goodison Road stand when I first came to the club and there were an awful lot of priests there, some of them with hip flasks, and that was because of the Catholic connection with Peter, Tommy Eglington, Tommy Clinton and Don Donovan.'

Shortly before the domestic season ended, four Everton players were selected for the Ireland squad taking on the Netherlands in Dublin. Getting to the match had its challenges, though. Along with his three Irish clubmates, Peter dashed to Newcastle Airport from Roker Park immediately after their defeat to Sunderland. After an hour's wait, the foursome was advised that the specially chartered aircraft had developed a technical fault and was unserviceable. Just as the players had visions of spending the night in Newcastle, a small six-seater aircraft was flown up from Birmingham to collect them, reaching Dublin at half-past midnight. Any drowsiness the next day was shrugged off and the Irish defeated the Dutchmen 1–0.

Four weeks later, on 28 May, Peter reached the landmark of a quarter-century of appearances for his country in a 2–1 defeat to World Cup holders West Germany in Hamburg. In doing so, he became the second player (after Johnny Carey) to be awarded a silver shamrock ornament. Each of the six leaves of the shamrock was engraved with details of the matches he had appeared in. It remains a prized family possession.

That coveted FAI trophy left a lasting impression on eight-year-old Evertonian Bernie Pedder, who in 1955 was living on Kensington Terrace. 'One of my earliest memories is of the day my mum said, "Come on, we're going somewhere," and she walked us down to a store called TJ Hughes. When we got in Peter Farrell was on a small stage giving a talk about his reminiscences of playing for Ireland. On the table next to him was this ornate silver shamrock he had got for making 25 appearances – it has stuck in my memory.'

Remarkably, although 33 when the 1955/56 season got underway, the Dubliner was an ever-present through the campaign, which ended in a mid-table position on a modest 40 points. Due to avoiding significant injury (a broken jaw apart) and his unrivalled dedication, the Irishman had an amazingly consistent appearance record through the years since his arrival a decade previously. After his debut season (in which he had arrived carrying an injury), he never made fewer than 37 league appearances in the campaigns that followed. The five-foot-eight wing-half was now stockier (reportedly weighing 12st. 7lb) than when he had moved from Shamrock Rovers to Everton, but he had never been blessed with exceptional pace, so did not have it to lose. He would continue to compensate for that lack of speed with his accurate passing with either foot and an uncanny positional sense that took him to the right place at the right moment to make an interception or be unmarked to receive a pass. His skill was equalled by his wonderful temperament and influence on teammates.

On the international front, with no World Cup qualifiers, matches were thin on the ground, but the hosting of Yugoslavia at Dalymount on 19 October 1955 caused a storm of controversy. Archbishop of Dublin John Charles McQuaid called on the FAI to cancel the fixture. His considerable influence had seen the FAI twice decline offers from Yugoslavia to send a team to Ireland. He considered the staging of the match as a tacit endorsement of President Josip Tito's Communist regime, which had imprisoned and put under subsequent house arrest a Zagreb archbishop, who had a record of being accommodating to the fascists during the Second World War.

On this occasion, the archbishop felt slighted as he had not been consulted by the FAI before the fixture was announced. Nonetheless, with plans for the match well advanced, the FAI leadership was not to be swayed by the representations. McQuaid then called on Catholic football supporters to boycott the match. RTE was forced to abandon plans to broadcast the fixture over the radio when members of the sports department refused to work on it; the tipping point was Philip Greene declining do his customary commentary duties.

In spite of the archbishop's appeal and some protests in the vicinity, 22,000 spectators did pass through the Dalymount turnstiles and saw Peter lead out the hosts. The controversy over the staging of the fixture saw a number of high-profile Irish politicians give it a miss, while the national anthems had to be played from records over the Tannoy system in the absence of the Army Number One Band.

Tito, over a thousand miles away, had the satisfaction of his team coming away from Dublin with a 4–1 win.

The Yugoslavia match coincided with Johnny Carey being asked to fill the role of team manager for the Irish national side on a part-time basis. His 'day job' was with

Leading Ireland out to play Spain in 1955. Everton clubmate Jimmy O'Neill follows Peter out of the tunnel.

Blackburn Rovers. Like his predecessor, Alex Stevenson, Carey faced the challenge of having precious little time with his players before an international fixture. He would seek to mitigate the issue by writing to all of the squad members a week before each match with his thoughts on the game plan. Below is an abridged version of what he sent (on headed Blackburn Rovers notepaper) to the players before the subsequent match, against Spain in late November:

> *I am sure that I will have your earnest co-operation and support, and look forward to working with you on Sunday. It is most unfortunate that we cannot be together for a few days prior to this important match, so that we could pool our ideas and get some teamwork into our play. We shall, however, have a pre-match talk at the Gresham Hotel before we leave for Dalymount.*
>
> *The continental players are extremely good when they are given plenty of room to work in. Therefore, it is important that we cut down the gaps in the centre of the field*

as much as possible. We must try to play quick, accurate football with the ball kept on the ground. Try to keep the ball moving by every player running into open spaces. If there is no-one to pass to, then don't be frightened to hold onto the ball.

When we are on the defence, I would like our wingers to come back well into our half of the field to pick up the clearances. Above all, lads, we must try to use the ball and avoid the aimless kick, which will get us nowhere. This applies to Jimmy O'Neill, as well, but the players must give Jimmy the chance to throw the ball out to them by moving into open space. I always consider that a team is playing well when they finish off their own attacking movements, so shoot at every available opportunity.

Spain is a good team, but not better than ours, if we play the football we are capable of.

Good luck lads; see you Sunday.

Very sincerely,

Jack Carey.

Working to the Carey game plan, Ireland shared the spoils with the Spaniards, 2–2.. Ironically, in spite of the Iberian nation being ruled by a fascist-leaning dictatorship under Franco, there had been none of the machinations experienced in the build-up to the Yugoslavia match.

16
CHANGES AT GOODISON

In February 1956, the skipper made his 400th senior appearance for the Toffees, narrowly beating Liverpool's own stalwart, Billy Liddle, to the mark. That outing, at Goodison Park, was capped by scoring the winner against Chelsea to send the Blues through to an FA Cup quarter-final. In his weekly newspaper column Peter wrote: 'It was such a long time since I scored that I had nearly forgotten what I felt like. Still the long wait was worthwhile but most of the credit for the goal must go to Brian Harris, Wally Fielding and Eddie Wainwright for their part in the move leading up to my shot.'

Liverpool and Manchester City were contesting one of the other fifth round ties that afternoon. At full-time, when word reached the Goodison crowd that the Mancunians had triumphed over the Reds, hundreds of excited youngsters dashed on to the pitch, whooping with joy and ready to mob Everton in general and Farrell in particular. One invader was downed by a police officer and tempers flared. In the end Peter just about survived his mobbing and must have been glad to reach the dressing room, where Cliff Britton was waiting to shake his hand.

In the days that followed, many Evertonians approached Peter in the street to offer congratulations and express their delight that Everton would not have to face Liverpool in the next round. He disagreed, as he relished a derby match and also felt some sympathy for Billy Liddell, the Reds' forward having been denied by the referee blowing for full time just as the Scot was in the act of scoring what would have been an equaliser.'

Six days after the elation of progression to a cup semi-final, Peter and his comrades were stunned by the news that Cliff Britton was quitting as the club's manager. There had been tension rumbling between Britton and several club directors for some months over what the former perceived to be interference in team affairs. Matters came to a head when the directors, unbeknown to Britton, appointed Harold Pickering as a stand-in manager for the close season to oversee club affairs in England while the manager and squad were on tour in North America. Taking umbrage, Britton walked out on the club. A war of words followed, conducted through the local newspapers, which did the club and its erstwhile manager no favours. Ernest Green was collateral damage; an ally of Britton, he resigned as chairman (albeit remaining a director) and was replaced by Dick Searle. Searle, who had returned to the board in 1953, two years after being voted off, had been less well disposed towards the manager, believing that too much authority had been ceded to him.

A quiet, private man, who felt players should not consume alcohol, Britton was viewed by some players to be a distant, somewhat aloof, character. However, there had always been a deep sense of trust and understanding between the manager and his captain of six seasons. This was further cemented when they made good on their promise of getting the Toffees promoted back to the First Division after the deep hurt and humiliation of relegation in 1951. There can be little doubt that Britton's departure was met with a mixture of shock and sadness by the Irishman. Nonetheless, as a senior professional at the club, he had to put these feelings to one side for the sake of his clubmates.

A subcommittee of three directors (Messrs T.C. Nuttall, C.E. Balmforth and F. Micklesfield) was appointed to deal with all matters relating to the playing staff until a new manager could be recruited. Peter and one or two other senior professionals on the Blues' books would be invited to have some input at midweek meetings with the directors. The captain would disclose to his teammates that one board member's grasp of tactics went no further than exclaiming: 'Give him a kick.'

Having defeated Bolton Wanderers at Goodison Park, 1-0, the squad headed to Buxton for a training camp in preparation for the big cup tie the following Saturday. There, the visiting Ranger reported: 'Peter Farrell, the captain, has been a tower of strength to his colleagues and has assured T.C. Nuttall and C. Balmforth, the directors in charge of the party, that nobody need have any doubts about the players pulling out every ounce of endeavour at Maine Road today.' Peter told the journalist: 'I think we have an excellent chance of victory. We know that City are a good side, they will present us with a very tough problem, but our supporters can rely on us to do our utmost from the word go. We have been a very happy party all week and whatever the result may be, if we do not get through it will not be for want of a valiant effort.' Peter asked Ranger to relay thanks, in his newspaper column, to the many people who had written to him and other members of the team wishing them the best of luck.

While at the Derbyshire spa town training camp, Peter was spotted quietly puffing on his pipe by Manchester City's Welsh international star Roy Paul and Arthur Walmsley of the *Evening Chronicle*. They got into conversation, with Peter reliving the acute disappointment he had felt when Everton lost the 1953 semi-final to Bolton Wanderers. Then, he turned to Paul, and with an impish grin said, 'That's not going to happen this year, Roy.'

And so to Maine Road, scene of The Toffees' FA Cup semi-final defeat to Bolton Wanderers three years previously, and a loss to Liverpool at the same stage three years prior to that. In the match build up, Peter used his *Liverpool Echo* column to make a surprising confession: 'Despite the fact that a League championship triumph is a prouder achievement from the point of view of skill that a Wembley victory I think that most footballers would rather a Cup winners medal than a League one. I know I would although either would be very welcome.'

Having arrived from the Peak District at the stadium, Peter, along with teammates Eric Moore and Tommy E. Jones, were greeted by a tremendous roar from the vociferous Everton contingent on the terraces when they entered the field to inspect the turf. When the Toffeemen came out in tracksuits ten minutes before the start they received another raucous welcome.

Peter won the coin toss and elected to defend the Moss Side goal in the first half. Determined to taste cup joy at Maine Road after the bitter disappointment experienced previously, Everton were fast out of the traps. Bert Trautmann, the German goalkeeper who had been brought from St Helens Town to Manchester by former Everton coach Jock Thomson, spared City's blushes on several occasions but was powerless to stop a Jimmy Harris strike, after the Birkenhead man was set free by Brian Harris in the 27th minute.

Roy Paul confessed to being amazed that his team only conceded one goal in the first half, and put much of the Toffees dominance down to their wing-halves: 'For 45 minutes, Everton played superb push-and-run football with the wing-halves, Peter Farrell and Cyril Lello, working like demon stokers, keeping the fires of enthusiasm working with a stream of passes.' The sports reporter, Ranger, meanwhile, described the venerable wing-half pair as 'keeping up the good work indefatigably'.

Summing up the opening 45 minutes in his *Liverpool Echo* column Peter wrote: 'In the first half the Blues gave one of the best displays of quick moving accurate football that I have seen in my ten years with the club. Our forward line has been criticized for not producing sufficient shots to round off their brilliant outfield moves. In this game and particularly in the first half the lads produced enough shots on the target to have given the Blues a substantial lead under ordinary circumstances. But on this occasion, we encountered Bert Trautmann at his brilliant best.'

With a solitary goal to show for their dominance in the first half, it was inevitable that some jitteriness would creep into Everton's play. Conversely, City, geed up by a team talk during the break and the support of much of the 76,129, crowd found their bite and rhythm. Peter's explanation for Everton playing second fiddle to City in the second half was not an overly defensive approach but a change from a sharp pass and move game to a carrying game by the Everton players, which gave opposing players the opportunity to put some hefty challenges in and win back possession. In spite of ceding control of the play, Everton defended resolutely until the 69th minute when Joe Hayes got his head a curling free-kick delivered by Roy Paul which was just out of the reach of Jimmy O'Neill in the Everton goal. Six minutes later, Roy Paul's compatriot Roy Clarke whipped in a cross from the left which was met by Bobby Johnstone who bulleted a header past Everton's Irish goalkeeper.

Everton, although reeling from the double whammy, never gave up, as Leslie Edwards described: 'Jones and Tansey were always playing as though their lives depended on it and Moore and the wing-half backs, too, never ceased in their efforts to pull the game round.' At the death they nearly forced an equaliser from three corners in the final minute but City held out. Having thanked their supporters the dejected players trudged of the pitch; great sportsman that he was, Peter wasted little

With Mabel for company and wise counsel, Peter was a guest judge at this beauty content, most likely at New Brighton. He was joined by former Everton clubmate, Joe Mercer, who was wearing his Arsenal club blazer for the occasion

94

Watched by Everton teammates and coaches, Peter and Tommy receive their long service benefit cheques in 1956

time in visited the home dressing room and congratulating the City players on their victory and progression to the next round of the competition. 'Everton fought magnificently. They lost magnificently' was the *Daily Post's* pithy summary. In his *Liverpool Echo* column a few days later, Peter wrote:

> *It was a very disappointed Everton side that trooped back into the dressing room after the game. Still, some consolation in defeat was the knowledge that we went out fighting, right to the end. I should like to take this opportunity of thanking Everton supporters not only for their vocal efforts but also for the kind letters that the members of the side have received during the week, praising the team display at Maine Road. It is easy to sing a side's praise in victory, and a little more difficult but all the more appreciated in defeat, it is acts like these, plus the great vocal effects of our thousands of loyal supporters, that make us all proud to be Evertonians. Here's hoping that some day before my playing days are over the Blues will give their fans something really to shout about in the honours list.*

Roy Paul would go on to lift the trophy for City. Peter, meanwhile, had to lead his side out again at Maine Road just four days later for a league fixture. Psychologically and physically drained, Everton fell to a 0–3 defeat, followed by further losses against Sunderland and Huddersfield Town. Although never threatened with relegation, Ranger noted that this was a team 'sliding, sliding, sliding' as it won a mere three of the final ten league fixtures of the season. That said, the skipper showed little sign of easing off. In the defeat to the Terriers, in which Dave Hickson netted against his former club, the *Daily Post* commented on Peter's efforts at left-half (he had been switched there due to Cyril Lello's absence, after a run of 150 consecutive appearances): 'If anything, the Everton captain was more effective than usual in his new position, and it was nothing to see him stem a raid in his own goalmouth and a minute later be up assisting his forwards. Indeed, it was from the centre-forward position that he set Fielding in motion on one occasion with a finely angled headed pass that was not taken advantage of by the inside man.'

A few weeks later, the *Echo* heaped similar praise on the evergreen player, in the defeat of Cardiff City: 'Though devoting much time to prompting his attack, Farrell was never once found wanting in defence and covered more ground than any other player on the field.'

With little to play for, the club blooded several young players in first team football. Welshman Graham Williams had been signed after the two defeats to Manchester City and was soon tried in place of Eglington on the left wing. Albert Harris, George Kirby and Ken Birch also got their first tastes of First Division football. At the conclusion of a hard-fought draw away to Sheffield United, Peter gave debutants Kirby and Birch encouraging pats on the back to recognise their efforts.

With the domestic season over, the Blues finishing in 15th place in the division, the squad played a match at Goodison against Brazilian opposition in the form of Vasco De Gama. It ended with a 6–3 win for the hosts and warm applause for the

Everton players and coach Charlie Leyfield combining golf with football on the 1956 tour of North America

visitors at the final whistle. Their continental tactical approach was something that caught Peter's eye, although he held strong reservations about its practicality in British football: 'You may have noticed that the visitors attacking formation was something on the same style of Manchester City's, with four forwards staying up-field even when their defence was on the collar. There are varying opinions on a system such as this, but in my opinion it throws a terrible lot of work on the defence, particularly if the opposition is dictating the play.'

There was to be no rest for the Toffees' players, as next up was a month's trip to North America – the tour which had precipitated the managerial crisis in late February. Prior to their departure, the board confirmed the appointment of Ian Buchan as the club's head coach. In a change of direction, the directors had dispensed with the position of manager, instead choosing to retain some of the powers previously held by Cliff Britton. Between coach and directors, Harold Pickering would act as the administrative officer. A left-field choice by Everton, Buchan had no experience as a player or coach in professional football. The Scot was a physical training expert who had been teaching prospective PE teachers at Loughborough College.

Buchan's requirement to serve his notice in Leicestershire meant he would not be joining up with the squad for the tour across the Atlantic. The Everton party travelled by train to Southampton before embarking on Cunard's *Queen Elizabeth* ocean liner. Mercifully, the six-day voyage to New York was a smooth one, with few reports of sea-sickness. In the absence of a manager on the trip, director Ernest Green asked Peter to keep an eye on his teammates. Every morning there was training session on deck, which Green would watch, complimenting the lads on appearing fit and sharp. Unlike Peter, he was not wise to the fact that most of the lads hadn't been to bed and were feeling the worse for wear.

Disembarking in the Big Apple, the tour party was welcomed by representatives of the American Soccer League and, the following day, met the city's mayor. The trip to his office was made in seven cars, with a smooth passage through downtown city traffic being assured by the shrieking sirens of the police motorcycle escort.

The ten-match programme began in Newark, New Jersey, with a fixture against a local Portuguese–Polish XI. Next was a thumping 7–0 defeat of an American Soccer League XI. The ASL goalkeeper, Orlando Jorge, was impressed by the side which put seven past him: 'I have never seen anything that compares with that team. They're great. Everton players are in perfect condition. They run, run for 90 minutes. And can they ever handle the ball; their teamwork is perfect. They make short, precision passes. They put the ball right on the other guy's toe. And they kick it like a cannon shot. When they get in range – brother, can they put it in the corner.'

In a subsequent match in Boston, the – perhaps hyperbolic – local newspaper report described the Toffees as being 'as nimble-footed a clan of musclemen as ever appeared on the chewed-up Franklin Park pitch'. The only defeat was a narrow 0–1

Peter performs his pre-match captain's duties in the USA

loss to West German side Schwaben (the Everton programme report of the tour described the opponents as 'vigorous and dirty' in their play. The nearest Everton came to scoring was when Peter dribbled half the length of the field but hit the post as the German goalkeeper ran out to narrow the angle.

While in New York, the tourists from Liverpool were blown away when shown the city's stunning sites, and were also given guided tours of a brewery and the Radio City Music Hall. The Blues skipper made the acquaintance of Sam Chedgzoy – the legendary Everton and England outside-right who had won the league title in 1914/15 and, a decade later, helped Dixie Dean to settle in at Goodison Park. He had emigrated to North America shortly afterwards and made a home in Canada. Always one to keep tabs on his former club, Chedgzoy had made the trip south to watch a match, but ended up disappointed, as Peter explained later in his *Echo* column:

> Sam flew 500 miles to New York to see Everton play Aberdeen, only to learn that the game had been postponed owing to incessant rain. Despite his disappointment in not seeing the Blues in action, Sam assured me that the journey had been well worthwhile, and he had a lot of reminiscing to do with directors Mr. Green and Mr. Sharp about the old days, and he had many questions as to the whereabouts and welfare of some of his former colleagues. Before leaving, the former Everton winger asked me through this column to give a message of good wishes to all Evertonians

who gave him such great encouragement from the terraces some years ago.

From New York the party flew to St Louis, where Peter, fellow player Jimmy Harris, trainer Charlie Leyfield and club secretary Bill Dickinson appeared on a local television station broadcast, prior to their match with a local Catholic Youth XI (sadly, the interview has not re-emerged). A train ride took the Toffeemen to Chicago for their next fixture. Peter and Tommy had, for many years, delighted in confusing people as to which of them was older. After the match in Chicago, at the post-match reception, he was somewhat puzzled by the effusive praise for his performance in what was a fairly meaningless fixture. It transpired that Eglington had made it known to spectators that Peter was 44, 12 years older than his true age.

The tour continued in Canada with three exhibition matches against Scottish opponents Aberdeen. Ironically, in light of the opposition, on touching down in Vancouver the Everton side was welcomed by four city police and pipers in Stuart tartan. The first match, in the British Columbian city, was notable for being played under floodlights – still a novelty for British footballers (Goodison Park's lights would be installed in 1957).

Peter thoroughly enjoyed the tour, seeing a new continent for the first time. Moreover, it proved quite lucrative for him: 'The beauty of that was that we were on a four pounds win bonus and the teams weren't very good!' In his newspaper column he recounted meeting many exiled Merseysiders – most of whom professed to missing their regular dose of soccer at either Goodison or Anfield. He also bumped into Canadian player Gordon 'Gogie' Stewart, who had spent the 1953/54 season on Merseyside, playing for Everton's reserve team. Having declined the offer of a further season at Goodison Park, Stewart was now back home and decked out in a ten-gallon black hat and coloured windbreaker to greet his erstwhile comrades.

The two British teams wrapped up the tour with the rescheduled match against Aberdeen, played in New York on 17 June. The airline BOAC held up the departure of their Boeing Stratocruiser service across the Atlantic as the side dashed to the airport after the match. The aircraft was due to refuel at Prestwick and land at Manchester but was forced by the inclement weather to proceed directly to London. At London Airport the players rushed to change dollars to sterling so they could phone their wives and relatives with the news that they would be late home. An aircraft was then laid on by the airline to get the squad back to Merseyside. Finally arriving at Liverpool's Speke Airport on the evening of 18 June, Peter caught the night boat to Dublin to join up with his family.

Bill Dickinson, the Everton secretary who oversaw the tour, said that it had been 'very, very successful'. He continued: 'The United States standard of football is not very high, but the Canadian standard is a little better. Of the native teams we met, the Chicago side were the best of the bunch.'

One member of the tour party that summer had been Matt Woods, a towering centre-half. Having proved unable to dislodge Tommy E. Jones from the team, he moved to Blackburn Rovers a few months later. Typical of his approach to being the Toffees' skipper, Peter sent a telegram to Woods before he debuted for Rovers, stating, simply: 'Best wishes and good luck – from Peter and the boys.'

17
HEADING TOWARDS THE EXIT

On 18 July 1956, a month after his return from North America, Peter reported for the first day of training in the Ian Buchan era. The Scot, at the request of the Everton chairman, addressed a few remarks to the players on meeting them for the first time. On behalf of his colleagues, Peter – who retained the captaincy – extended a warm welcome to the new head coach, assured him of wholehearted co-operation and wished him a long and happy career with the club.

The players soon found themselves immersed in Buchan's more scientific approach to training and conditioning. The intensive regime, with a mixture of running and gym work, came as a culture shock, but Peter told Ranger that he was impressed with the fitness progress made: 'If anybody had told me ten days ago that I would do that [20 quarter-mile laps of Bellefield] I wouldn't have believed them. Our coach knows his stuff all right and everybody is getting much more enjoyment out of the pre-season preparation than we thought possible. To be candid I never imagined I should relish training as much as I have this last week or so. It has been quite an eye-opener.'

He took up a similar theme in his weekly *Echo* column:

During the past four weeks under our new coach Ian Buchan, all the boys at Goodison have undergone a very strenuous yet interesting schedule of training. In our new gymnasium under the Gwladys Street Stand we have shed quite a lot of perspiration in our circuit training and weight-lifting. We have also devoted much time endeavouring to speed up our movement in this respect with the aid of the stop-watch. Mr. Bu-

The Everton team in the 1956/57 season – Peter's last as a first team player. The goalkeeper is Albert Dunlop, one of surprisingly few Merseysiders to appear between the posts for the Toffees. Head coach Ian Buchan is on the far right of the back row

chan and his staff discovered that we have quite a few speed merchants in our ranks. We have also devoted considerable time [with] the ball, skills and the different phases of our time. It will be interesting to see how this new form of training will benefit us both individually and collectively. Time will tell and I am sure all the hard work of the past month will have the boys right on their toes for the task ahead of us in giving 100 per cent effort in the cause of Everton.

Buchan's approach was decidedly innovative (circuit training was virtually unheard of in English football, at this point), but not welcomed by all of the senior pros. Weight training was anathema to the spindly and ageing Wally Fielding, who was not averse to grumbling about it. Goalkeeper Jimmy O'Neill was certainly unimpressed: 'He [Buchan] was a total fitness fanatic. All of our work was geared towards raising our levels of fitness. He did not believe in using the ball much during the week. Give him weight training and sprinting against the clock and he was in his element, but as a football manager ... well, he left a lot to be desired.'

The Scot's lack of tactical acumen and, in some cases, the moderate quality of players in the side, hampered performances. Brian Labone, a future Everton captain but a junior squad member at the time, recalled: 'Ian Buchan was an absolute fitness fanatic. Everton were the fittest team in the league, but we couldn't play football. He was strictly a coach, never a player, whereas Johnny Carey [his eventual replacement] was the other way round.' Buchan was not helped by the appointment of Harry Wright, a former army physical trainer instructor, as his sidekick, rather than an experienced football coach who could have provided the tactical acumen the Scot lacked.

The season had started worryingly poorly before a win was achieved at the eighth attempt. Perhaps, by this point, the Buchan fitness regime was reaping dividends, as evidenced by the Toffees enjoying a 5–2 victory at Old Trafford in late October. In the week leading up to another big fixture, at home to Arsenal, Peter received a call at Goodison Park from a woman whose husband, a life-long Evertonian, was in a Liverpool hospital in his last days of life. She felt that a visit from the Everton players might give him a lift. The team did visit hospitals every month, anyway, but the wheels were put in motion for the ailing man to see his heroes one final time. Arriving at the bedside, Peter introduced himself and expressed his hope that the man would recover enough to get to a few more games at Goodison Park. The response, accompanied by a weak smile came back: 'Ah, Peter, I will not be back watching Everton again, I am a dying man. But there is one thing you can do for me before I die. I want to lie here on Saturday afternoon and listen to my radio and hear you hammer Arsenal. Just hammer Arsenal, Peter – that's all.'

The Toffees did just that, unexpectedly battering the Gunners 4–0, with Peter scoring the third goal. Peter saw the sick man's wife a few days later and expressed his hope that the result had proved the fillip needed. She relayed the sad news that he had passed away on the Friday night before the match; however, he died thrilled to have spent time chatting with his football heroes

It may have been this Arsenal match Peter had in mind when recalling, in 1982, the supporters' commitment to the cause. The Blues were experimenting with a bluff when defending their box from Gunners' freekicks. On the first occasion, Peter would look across the defensive line and shout 'okay' – upon which the blue-shirted players would move out together and catch the forwards offside.

The next time the visitors had a free-kick in a similar danger area, Peter called out, 'Same again, lads.' Arsenal fully expected the Everton defence to move out, but Peter's call was code for them to remain where they were. The Gunners' forwards moved away from goal in anticipation of the attempt to be caught offside. This left the Blues with time and space to clear their lines.

Three days later, a supporter approached the skipper on Goodison Road and exclaimed: 'Jesus, Peter, didn't that offside trap work beautifully?' He went on to explain how he was stood in the Bullens Road Paddock, in line with the edge of the 18-yard box. When he heard Peter shout 'okay' to his teammates, the supporter turned to his mates in the Paddock and shouted, 'Ready, lads.' When Arsenal took their kick, as one, the Paddock spectators moved out in unison with the Toffees defence. Peter reflected: 'What amused me most about the whole incident was that this same support could not understand why I laughed so much at his description of his free-kick. He thought it was totally normal that a whole Paddock section of the supporters should see themselves as active participants in the game. The supporters were like that. They lived and died talking and thinking Everton.'

With some stability established, a 15th position in the league in the 1956/57 season was achieved. Although Peter may have been publicly effusive in his praise for what Ian Buchan brought to training at Everton, years later, in conversation with Joe Dodd (author of a book about footballers from the Dún Laoghaire area), he was more circumspect about the Scot's abilities as a head coach. Harbouring reservations about the depth of Buchan's knowledge of football tactics and managerial abilities, he probably also sensed that he was on borrowed time in the side. After Cliff Britton's era of excessive loyalty to long-serving first-teamers who were some way past their peak, Buchan made a concerted effort to promote promising youngsters who had been stuck in the Central League (reserve) side. Meanwhile, Graham Williams being selected on the left wing late in the season signalled that Tommy Eglington's final days at Everton were looming.

Reflecting on the season in his *Echo* column, Peter mused: 'I suppose from an Everton viewpoint we have done nothing to shout about.' For balance, he went on to point out how the side had rallied after an abysmal start and that youngsters like Albert Dunlop, Ken Birch, Ken Rea, Eddie Thomas, Derek Temple, William Haughey and Graham Williams would only improve in the next season, after being given their game time by Buchan. Top of the list of Peter's highlights was that superb performance at Old Trafford which saw the Toffees beat the Busby Babes 5–2. 'One of the greatest displays of football I have ever seen from an Everton side,' was how Peter described the performance. Sadly, having set up a cup tie against the Red Devils by scoring a late winner against West Ham, Peter was dejected after a 1–0 defeat at Old Trafford in the fifth round: 'I well remember the look of disappointment on the faces of the lads, as we trooped off Old Trafford having been beaten 1–0 in the Cup by Manchester United. We weren't disgraced by any means, but this was poor consolation for the fact that yet another chance of a Wembley appearance had gone begging.'

The captain finished his review of the season with a tribute to the supporters, with whom he continued to enjoy a close bond: 'So here's wishing all football enthusiasts all the best for the close season with a special word of thanks to those loyal supporters of the Blues who follow us through thick and thin, and especially to

Taking training with the US Air Force team based at Burtonwood, one of several coaching assignments Peter undertook in his spare time during his playing career

those diehards who rarely miss an away game irrespective of how the side is faring. We all certainly appreciate your great support and loyalty.'

Peter had found time to combine skippering Everton with coaching noted local amateur outfit Liverpool Ramblers, a club co-founded by Bruce Ismay of White Star shipping line fame. Since the mid-1930s, the Toffees had been supplying players to take evening coaching sessions. Over the years, Hunter Hart, Alex Stevenson, Gordon Dugdale, Maurice Lindley and Harry Potts had performed these duties. When the latter departed Goodison for Wolves, where he would be a scout, it fell to Peter to take the reins. His reward, aside from the satisfaction of helping the local community and getting coaching experience, was an invitation to the club's annual hot-pot evening.

Somehow, he also found the time to coach the US Air Force's 'Gunners' football team, based at the Burtonwood airfield, located between Liverpool and Warrington. Every Wednesday afternoon, the servicemen, many of them with European heritage – hence their passion for soccer – changed into their kit and were put through their paces by the amiable Irishman. Peter had this to say when asked by the *Echo* about his protégés: 'It seemed strange to me when the Gunners asked me to coach them in what is traditionally a European sport, but after a few sessions with the boys I saw they had a lot of potential. Most important, they had a good team sense. The one thing they do not lack is confidence.'

Peter's 28th selection for the Republic of Ireland side came on 8 May 1957, a World Cup qualifying match away to England. It would be the veteran's first

The September 1957 edition of Charles Buchan's Football Monthly carried an illustration of Peter leading the Toffees onto the pitch (the second time he had been a cover star). Ironically, at the time of publication, Peter had lost his place in the side and was soon to be on the move to Tranmere Rovers

appearance at Wembley – partial recompense for narrowly missing out on two FA Cup finals there. He wrote, in his *Liverpool Echo* column:

> *One of my greatest thrills of the season was last Sunday morning when I picked up the paper and learned that I had been chosen to captain Eire at Wembley next Wednesday. Nearly all footballers have an ambition to play at Wembley and believe me, I am no exception. You can imagine my feeling when I learned that I was not only to achieve my great ambition, but also to captain my country [at] one of the most famous stadiums in the world. I only wish that Tommy Eglington were trotting out next Wednesday with Don Donovan and myself to get that much desired Shamrock for his twenty-fifth appearance.*

Making his debut in the Irish goal that day was Alan Kelly, who three decades later would coach Everton's goalkeepers, as would his son, Alan Kelly Jr, in the 2020s. Unfortunately, the 35-year-old wing-half had a poor game in a 5–1 defeat at the home of English football. He was omitted for the return fixture at Dalymount Park 11 days later, bringing the curtain down on 11 years of dedicated service to his country. In that time, he had captained his national side 12 times, scored three goals and had the distinction of being the first player to make a substitute appearance in Dublin for his country. Most importantly, as a proud Irishman, he had left nothing on the pitch and done much to inspire his compatriots through his positivity and example-setting.

No longer required by his national side, he joined the Toffees on their post-season tour of Ireland – a great opportunity for Evertonians living in Ireland to see their captain without having to catch the ferry to Liverpool. At Dalymount, the Blues, with five Irishmen in the side, lost 2–4 to Shamrock Rovers, managed by Paddy Coad, before securing a 1–0 win over Glentoran at The Oval in Belfast.

Eight days later, six Everton Irishmen (Farrell, Eglington, O'Neill, Donovan, Sutherland and Meagan) turned out, for expenses only, for a Galway Select XI versus Shamrock Rovers at the Showground in Galway. They were captained by Con Martin, then of Waterford.

After 428 appearances since his arrival on Merseyside in 1946, 34-year-old Tommy Eglington made the short move to Tranmere Rovers of the Third Division North in the 1957 close season. His arrival on the Wirral coincided with the departure of former Ireland and Everton teammate Tommy Clinton, who was moving on from Rovers to Runcorn FC. Peter, without his close friend as a Toffees teammate for the first time in over 14 years, was confirmed as the Blues' captain for an eighth successive campaign.

In the pre-season Blues versus Whites match (contested between the expected first and reserve teams), Peter underwhelmed the watching Ranger by seemingly playing within himself. Ian Buchan concurred, as he sprung a surprise for the first league match of the season. Returning hero Dave Hickson (back at his beloved

Everton after spells at Aston Villa and Huddersfield Town) wore the number nine shirt once more, but Peter had to cede his number six shirt to Mick Meagan; Ken Birch was selected in the other wing-half position. Hearing the news, Ranger, in the *Echo*, paid tribute to the skipper on this significant changing of the guard: 'Farrell, despite his approach to the veteran stage, never let the team down last season. Many a time he was fighting back when others were ready to call it a day. Apart from his ability, Farrell's whole-hearted endeavour was always an inspiration.'

With the Blues having a strong start to the season, there was no opportunity for the veteran to regain his place, thus he remained stuck on 452 senior outings. In his *Liverpool Echo* column, he was generous in his praise for fellow Irishman Meagan: 'It was obvious that before long the Dublin lad would be staking a claim for inclusion in the first team. Good luck to you, Mick, you have got all the attributes it takes to make a great attacking wing-half-back.'

Peter was not one to sulk, instead attempting to perform a (non-playing) captain's role by urging on his clubmates from the touchline. Not all supporters appreciated his efforts, as he described in his *Echo* column:

> *During last Saturday's reserve game against Sheffield United, I was continually shouting encouragement to the lads, during the course of the game. Some of the fans in the Paddock seemed to take exception to hearing my voice on the field. Several times I heard remarks such as 'Keep your mouth shut Farrell – and let the kids play their own game.' I wonder what these people think I am trying to do. Put the youngsters off their game or what? Far from it. I consider it part of my duty as captain, no matter what team I am in, to help my teammates with vocal advice or to point out to them what they are doing wrong during the course of the game. The lads appreciate this, and realise I am only doing my duty. I know it is only a small minority of the fans who don't seem to realise this, so I would like to put their minds at ease by informing them that I shall continue in such a way as long as I am captain of an Everton side.*

As it transpired, his time as Everton captain – and at Everton, period – was nearly over. Come the end of September, Tranmere Rovers attempted to reunite Peter with Tommy Eglington. The Toffees readily gave permission for a formal approach, making it patently clear to the skipper that he was now considered expendable. Informal talks were held between the player and Wirral club but, after sleeping on it, the 35-year-old gave a polite 'thanks, but no thanks' message to the Prenton Park directorate, the drop in level being a factor. However, three days later, Rovers returned with the offer of a player-manager position, which was enough to sway Peter. Everton would receive £2,500 by way of compensation for the transfer.

Having signed on the dotted line on 4 October, watched by E. Blackburn, Tranmere's secretary-manager (who, much like Theo Kelly at Everton in 1948, would become purely the secretary from that point onwards), he used his final captain's column in the *Echo* to explain why he had made the difficult choice to leave his soul club:

IT'S A BIG WRENCH TO LEAVE GOODISON PARK

All good things eventually come to an end. For the first time since I joined Everton, over 11 years ago, I have been concerned during the past week, in talks regarding a move, and I have now decided to throw in my lot with Tranmere Rovers, for whom I signed last night as player-manager. I cannot hope to give Tranmere such lengthy service as I gave Everton, but I hope that the playing-time I still have left will be to Tranmere's advantage and that long before the end of the season they will have made certain of a place in the new national Third Division. My years at Goodison Park were very happy. Obviously, one cannot end such an association without a feeling of considerable regret. I leave many good friends behind me, but I will not be too far away, and I hope to make many more to compensate at Prenton Park. I would like to take this opportunity to thank all the Everton supporters for their wonderful encouragement, not only to me but to all the other past and present players, and to wish Don Donovan and the rest of the boys, not forgetting Chief Ian Buchan, the very best of good fortune.

18

THE IRISH ROVER

The town's newspaper, the *Birkenhead Advertiser and News,* **proclaimed the** new signing as a 'proud day' for Rovers and praised the perseverance of the club directors in getting the deal over the line. The new manager inherited a side that was only kept off the foot of the Third Division North table by goal average, with just seven points from the 12 opening fixtures. He went straight into the side as skipper at right-half in the weekend fixture against Southport. The 2–1 win prompted an 'Irish Eyes Were Smiling' headline in the local newspaper, with reporter Stuart Hooton commenting on the debutant: 'If he was nervous, he gave no clue, on the contrary, he appeared to be thoroughly enjoying himself.' With some excruciating punning, he also lapsed into 'Oirish' and described Peter as a 'darlin' bye'.

No sooner had Peter moved clubs than Everton were looking for him to vacate his club house on Thirlmere Drive. In fact, Tranmere Rovers made an approach to purchase the house for £1,800, so that Peter and family need not relocate, but they didn't follow it up. Instead, the Farrells settled in a larger semi-detached house on Carlaw Road on the Wirral, a ten-minute walk from Prenton Park.

It was there that daughter Sheila has one of her clearest childhood memories: 'At Eastertime, when I was around five years old, we'd have a houseful of chocolate eggs

THE LIFE AND TIMES OF PETER FARRELL

Mabel and Peter dressed to impress for a function

111

Player-manager Farrell taking training at Tranmere Rovers in the late 1950s (credit: Peter Bishop)

sent from supporters. They came in baskets with icing on – they seemed to be half the size of me. The hardest moment of my life was choosing which one I could keep – then a van came to collect the others and take them to an orphanage. My parents used to explain it all to me, but I didn't care, it was my saddest moment!'

For elder sister, Betty, it was in this period that she began to appreciate her father's fame: 'I remember that we were watching the news one night in Carlaw Road and they were showing a clip of a Tranmere match and Mum said: "That's your daddy on the television." The next minute he walked through the door and we couldn't understand how he could be in two places at once! I think that's when I realised that he was famous – but they never really talked about it at school.'

One other childhood memory remains imprinted on Betty's mind: 'I remember my parents going to the Lord Mayor's Ball in Liverpool. They got dressed up – Mum had made her own dress for it and Dad was in his dinner jacket. I remember thinking: "My God – they look amazing."'

Off the pitch, Peter made himself popular with the Tranmere faithful by writing a newspaper column and continuing to give his time freely for community organisations. One example was a speaking engagement at Runcorn AFC Members' Club at which he gave his views on British football and what could be done to improve it. He held the view that British football clubs and supporters had become too obsessed with winning rather than playing well – and had failed to note the rapid development of the game on the Continent and in South America. He went on to state that, tactics aside, strong team spirit and enthusiasm were a great basis for success. He also continued his Liverpool Ramblers coaching assignment, the Rovers board giving him permission to do so on the proviso that training was switched from Tuesday to Wednesday evenings in order to avoid any clash with matches. He would step down from the Ramblers at the conclusion of the 1957/58 season.

Having had an opportunity to assess his new team's style of play and the calibre of players, he made important tweaks to improve defensive resilience: 'Our full-backs were too square, so I had them doing much more covering. Another thing we did was to get our wingers to play much deeper.'

The supporters were also enamoured with the style of football he sought to bring to Prenton, no doubt influenced by over a decade at the 'School of Science'. Peter Bishop, in his book *Tranmere Rovers: The Complete Record*, states that the Farrell era produced the best pure football Prenton Park denizens had ever seen, which was reflected in a surge in numbers going through the turnstiles.

Early in his time at Tranmere, in a conversation with Frank Swift, the former Manchester City and England goalkeeper turned sports columnist, Peter acknowledged the debt he had to his former manager: 'I always consider myself as lucky to have been at Goodison during Cliff Britton's time there. I learned a lot from him and will be using a few of his tactical ideas here, as well as some of my own.' The move reunited Peter with 'Eggo' and the pair would regularly josh over the fact that Peter was now the boss. 'I would pull Tommy's leg about that,' chuckled Peter some years later. 'I often used to threaten him with the sack!'

There would be no immediate injection of new players to the squad. Instead, the new boss worked with the tools at his disposal and exerted his own influence on the pitch. He got an early taste of how football management can be a bizarre business when Blackpool made an approach for a player. With a small squad, he was reluctant to part with a player who, although he did not rate him highly and found him 'flash-looking', he felt was worth in the region of £2,000. Having intimated that he would not part with the player, he was stunned when the Seasiders came back with an offer of £8,000, which he was only too happy to accept.

Reinforcements eventually arrived in the shape of Liverpool centre-forward Antonio 'Tony' Rowley and Stockport County winger Ken Finney just before the March 1958 transfer deadline. Both proved astute additions to the Prenton Park roster as the club battled for a spot in what would be a newly formed national Third Division, replacing the two regional iterations of third-tier football. The match that could confirm qualification for the new division was against regional rivals Wrexham at Prenton Park, drawing a record Football League attendance for the club of 19,615. 'Never have fewer fathers been home for tea,' was the pithy comment from the local Birkenhead newspaper report.

In the event, Peter's team defeated the Dragons 2–1 on a famous night for the club. Late in the game, with Rovers 2–1 up, Peter was knocked out in a clash of heads when going up for an aerial challenge with Evans, the Wrexham centre-forward. Slumping to the ground, on the verge of passing out, he saw the ball rolling towards the Tranmere goal line. Little did he know that the ball had been comfortably claimed by the Rovers goalkeeper. It was only a few minutes after being revived that he appreciated that Rovers were still leading. Speeches were made in a crowded boardroom after the game – with club chairman C.W. Hodgson noting Peter's inspirational leadership. In reply, the manager shared the credit with the board, his players and the supporters' association. The team ended the season on 82 league goals, a figure that had been exceeded only once in the previous 22 years.

Life in the new national third tier meant that Tranmere and its supporters would have to quicky acclimatise to travelling the length and breadth of the country for away fixtures. Peter and Tommy Eglington would bring their experience to bear while Rowley, of Italian descent but born in Porthcawl, was in superb scoring form as the offensive spearhead. His 24 league goals in 36 outings pushed Rovers up the table and earned him international honours for the country of his birth. In October Peter celebrated a year in post, having made 46 consecutive appearances for the first team, amassing 55 points. A local journalist marked the anniversary by using his newspaper column to praise the 'stocky, chubby-faced Irishman' thus: 'Farrell is a fast-talking, friendly man. He is one of the unmistakable gentlemen of a sport that certainly cannot claim to be rich in this pleasant species.'

Reflecting on his first year at the helm of the Rovers, the manager said: 'I couldn't have been happier, here. I can't honestly say we've got a great team, because we haven't. But what we have got is a great team spirit, and that counts for an awful lot. Money can't buy you a contented mind. I've got to admit, I came here at the most opportune time – from my point of view, that is.'

The 1958/59 season saw a creditable seventh-place finish. Off the pitch, the club was looking to develop its facilities and had unveiled a new £15,000 stand in the autumn of 1958. However, the very modest budget for signings and wages would eventually see Rovers struggling near the foot of the table in the spring of 1960. In February of that year, Peter announced that he would be hanging up his boots and focusing fully on managing Rovers from the following summer. In spite of displays by the player-manager described by the local newspaper as 'lion-hearted', Tranmere went into the final few fixtures with relegation a distinct possibility. A hard-fought home win against Bury – Peter's last home league match – lifted Rovers out of the relegation zone. A point from the final fixture would be enough to guarantee safety. This was duly achieved on the following Saturday, 30 April, when the Wirral side went to already relegation-doomed Mansfield Town. Scoring after seven minutes, they went on to a 2–0 win and finished the season three points above relegated York City. This was the skipper's 573rd and last senior competitive match in English football. Also hanging up his boots that season had been Harold Bell, a legendary

Tranmere figure who had amassed 631 appearances – their paths would cross again within a year.

A few days later, Peter was able to bid farewell to Prenton Park as a player in more relaxed circumstances, in the benefit match against Ellesmere Port Town for long-serving Rovers full-back Derek Jones. Before the start of the second half, the players of both teams and match officials lined up round the centre-circle to salute their Irish manager. They linked hands while 'Auld Lang Syne' was played over the stadium loudspeakers.

Fate decreed that his final outing in a Tranmere shirt would be at Goodison Park, as the Wirral side would contest the Liverpool Senior Cup final with the Toffees. Stuart Hooton, reporting in the *Birkenhead News and Advertiser*, described the evening as a night of nostalgia and an 'unforgettable send off for Farrell'. According to Mike Charters, reporting on proceedings for the *Liverpool Echo* and *Evening Express*:

> The drama tinged with sadness, and the sense of occasion in Peter Farrell's appearance, overshadowed all else at Goodison Park last night. The facts are that Everton retained the Liverpool Senior Cup by defeating Tranmere Rovers 5–2, but the essential romance of the game was that 15,316 people turned up to pay their tribute to a man who has been a credit to professional football and now goes into full time management at Prenton Park with the good wishes of everyone. Mr. Farrell came onto the pitch between the two teams to a fine ovation, but the climax came at the end as hundreds of boys poured onto the ground to back-slap the night's hero down the tunnel for the last time. Then the man who played so many wonderful and valuable games for his two clubs, Everton and Tranmere, appeared in the directors' box to see Everton skipper Tom Jones receive the trophy and say a few words himself. I know he thanked everyone –and wished Everton well in the future – but the phrase I'll always remember was: 'I've reached the end of the road now.' In a playing sense, yes, Peter ... not, I'm sure, in football generally.

> It would have been the crowning touch if Peter could have led Tranmere to victory in his last match. But Everton's superior class and speed told in the end ... It was fitting that Farrell should end his career by a display in which he showed that the thought and craft is there as in his best days, even if the passing of the years has taken those vital yards off his speed. But he has left his own legacy to his team – the teaching of a top-class craftsman which was obvious in many of the fine touches his men showed and continued to try to do even when they were behind. The crowd appreciated the attempts to play cultured football even if they lacked the positional sense and know-how of the First Division opponents.

> The result didn't really seem to matter; we had gone to see the farewell of a great player – and he didn't let us down.

Peter's two eldest daughters, Betty and Pauline, recall going to the match. Betty asked her dad to wave to them as he ran out onto the pitch. He said that he could not, but he would pat down his hair with his right hand, his secret way of waving to them. Both were thrilled when they saw him doing that as he ran onto the Goodison pitch. After the match, the Everton Supporters' Club held a tribute to Peter in their City Road building (the former Coliseum cinema) and made a presentation in recognition of his footballing career on Merseyside.

Although relegation had been avoided and Peter was now able to focus solely on overseeing team affairs, a stormy club AGM underlined the concerns of shareholders as the club prepared for another season in the Third Division. Pertinent questions were asked, ranging from arrangements for signing players, training methods, team selection and the commitment of directors to attend second-team matches.

One innovation that summer was the use of David Locker – an Israeli coach, over in the UK to sit exams at Lilleshall – who took some training sessions and also gave Peter and his team insights into continental training methods and tactical approaches. Reportedly, the club's two goalkeepers, who had been glad to avoid a training session of pavement pounding around Birkenhead, instead found themselves undergoing an arduous Locker drill which had them repeatedly diving to either side to save imaginary shots, followed by doing several laps of the training pitch while juggling a ball.

A family recollection has it that Peter was forever grateful for a note of encouragement and offer of help, of advice, received from Huddersfield Town manager Bill Shankly when he took the reins at Tranmere in 1957. The Scot, who Peter had come up against when the Toffees took on Preston North End in the immediate post-war years, was appointed Liverpool manager in December 1959 with a brief to restore them to the top flight. Peter would later tell an Irish sports journalist that he had gone to see Shankly with a view to making an offer for one of his fringe players. He recalled the exchange thus: 'He brought me into his office, listened to me as I told him that I would be keen to buy his player and why I thought I needed him. Then, quite suddenly, he shook his head at me and said, "No, Peter, leave him alone." And with that he began making the international drinking gesture with his right hand, which indicated that the player in question had a drink problem. I took his advice and left that player well alone. I will never forget his [Shankly's] honesty.'

19

FROM THE WIRRAL TO WALES

The 1960/61 season would prove to be a tough one for all associated with Tranmere Rovers, none more so than the manager. The struggles on the pitch should have come as little surprise after the flirtation with relegation at the end of the previous campaign and the absence of quality in depth. With Peter having hung up his boots, Ralph Millington was appointed captain; he was joined in the side by new arrivals Willie Sinclair (ex-Huddersfield Town) and Stan Billington (ex-Everton).

Just two matches into the fixture programme, in the wake of a limp home performance against Swindon Town, Michel Chambers in the *Liverpool Echo* was pulling no punches about Rovers' prospects: 'If Rovers cannot make an immediate and drastic improvement, I forecast nothing but trouble for them this season ... Peter Farell must find new men or, next best thing, try some of his other players.'

On the back of two subsequent defeats, the manager turned to Nigerian forward Elkanah Onyeali to lead the line in early September. The youngster, in England to study at Birkenhead Technical College, had written in vain to Liverpool and Everton asking for a trial. He subsequently came to the attention of the Rovers manager and was given a chance in three reserve-team matches. Having impressed, he was offered, and accepted, part-time pro terms.

Onyeali, who hailed from Port Harcourt is believed to be the first black African-born footballer to play first team first team football for any of Merseyside's big three professional clubs. He was also Tranmere's first player to come from beyond the British Isles. 'Al', as the press soon dubbed him, started brightly, scoring twice on his league debut – a 4–3 defeat of Bournemouth and Boscombe, Rovers' first win in five attempts that season. He followed that up two days later with a further strike in a 2–1 defeat of Southend United.

However, studies came first for the promising forward, leading to logistical challenges of getting him to play in midweek matches. Having played in an evening match in Torquay, he travelled back overnight by train, so as to be available for his evening classes the next day. He was then driven down to Walsall for the Saturday match by a club director, linking up with his clubmates who had stayed in the Midlands for two nights. It is little surprise that, due to inexperience, lack of physical presence, absences when visiting his homeland and juggling studies with football, Onyeali faded from the first-team picture in December and was released at the end of the season.

In the opening months of the season, five goals were shipped to Halifax Town and Torquay, six to Grimsby Town and seven to Bury. A humiliating 2–9 away defeat to QPR on 3 December – in which the manager compared his defence to an open floodgate – was followed by a midweek FA Cup exit at the hands of York City.

It was imperative that the three-month winless streak at home was broken when Notts County came to Prenton Park on 10 December. Alas, a 2–3 defeat to the Magpies proved to be the final straw. The following Sunday morning, Peter met the club directors and a parting of the ways was agreed. For sentimental reasons, he managed to negotiate to remain in post for a Monday evening League Cup fixture against Everton; therefore, the announcement of his imminent departure was held back. The cup match was postponed at a late hour due to fog and the state of the pitch, so the news of the managerial change broke on the Tuesday morning. There was no rancour; the *Birkenhead Advertiser and News* described Peter as a great player for Rovers, blessed with 'wonderful agility, supreme anticipation and uncanny positional sense'. It wrote that in times of struggle, notably late in the 1959/60 season, 'he retained composure and skill'. Tranmere would recruit Walter Galbraith as their new manager, but the season would end in a 21st-place finish and relegation to the Fourth Division.

Reflecting in the 1980s, Peter was blunt when assessing how he had performed at Prenton Park and his own limitations: 'I was, frankly, not a success as a manager. I found it a very demanding job. By the end of my time, I was so worried about the way things were going that I couldn't sleep. Perhaps the best thing I did for the club was to help in getting their new stand built.' Peter would confess to his daughters that he enjoyed the camaraderie and 'craic' with teammates and found establishing the required distance from them to be a manager difficult. Coaching, without managerial responsibilities, would have suited him better.

In the wake of his departure from Tranmere, speculation in the Irish press linked Peter and Tommy Eglington, who carried on playing for Rovers until the spring of 1961, with Bray Wanderers. The former Shamrock Rovers duo was reportedly in talks about making an investment in the side with a view to getting it into the League of Ireland. Nothing transpired and by February 1961, Peter was dusting off the boots and making a playing comeback with Sligo Rovers. A steady start with a goal assist in a 3–3 draw against Cork Hibernians was followed by a heavy defeat at St Patrick's and a home loss to Waterford, in which Peter's free role as an inside-forward did not bear fruit. All parties agreed to draw the playing arrangement to a close at this point. However, Peter is in a very select group of stars, alongside Dixie Dean and Séamus Coleman, to represent both Everton and Sligo Rovers.

It was reported in the press that Peter would be taking up a position as a physical training instructor in the welfare department of a Merseyside factory. In fact, he was taken on by Girlings, a Bromborough-based manufacturer of vehicle brake components. His job as a progress chaser was to increase production. Thomas Connor, a work colleague, recalled, 'I spoke to him a lot, he was very friendly and always had time for a chat.'

Peter had been a regular spectator at Prenton Park and Goodison Park and, come the end of May 1961, he found a way back into football via a well-trodden path for veteran pros. Along the North Wales coast football had been booming thanks to clubs and their benefactors offering wages exceeding those permitted by the wage cap in the Football League. Plenty of stars in their twilight years, plus decent lower-tier players, were enticed by the financial incentives on offer. T.G. Jones is one of the best examples of a player tempted away from Everton, leading Pwllheli and District FC to new heights. Other former Toffeemen like Billy Higgins, Peter Corr and Norman Greenhalgh had also plied their trade at Bangor.

When Holyhead Town signed Peter as player-manager, it was agreed that he would commute to training sessions and matches from his home on the Wirral (where he would continue to work for Girlings). Once the top dogs in their league, the Harbourmen had been struggling prior to the Peter's arrival. One of his first signings was Harold Bell, the former Tranmere teammate of the new manager. In time, they would be joined by former Evertonians Jimmy Tansey and Tony McNamara plus a couple of young Irish footballers. The side already boasted the talents of Tommy Welsh, the Belfast man who had made his name as one of the most prolific goalscorers in Welsh football.

Gareth M. Davies, then a young man living in Holyhead, but later a chronicler of North Wales football, was one resident swept up in the excitement of the new appointment. Although a Wrexham supporter, his first senior football match as a spectator had been at Goodison Park in 1956, when the Toffees entertained Bolton Wanderers. Now, five years on, he was getting to see Everton's skipper from that day, leading his local team at the Recreation Ground. The Rec was known locally as Cae Mwd (Welsh for 'the mud field') – an apt nickname for the harbourside pitch which suffered from the wet conditions on the north-west tip of the island.

Although his pace and athleticism had diminished appreciably with the passage of time, Peter remained highly influential, drawing on his experience and leadership qualities. Davies recalls: 'I can still hear his voice, now, controlling everything. Although no longer at his best, then, he stood out like a beacon, prompting and probing. He was really well loved by the supporters.' Those coming to watch the former Ireland skipper were not just North Walians – a good number of supporters came by boat from Dún Laoghaire to Holyhead to see Peter in action, just as many had sailed to Liverpool when he was playing at Goodison Park.

The great gentleman that he was, Peter had never been booked in his entire career at Shamrock Rovers, Everton and Tranmere Rovers. However, that remarkable blemish-free streak was ended just a few months into his spell in Wales. In a feisty affair, Pwllheli and Holyhead went toe to toe. When a contentious decision went against the Harbourmen, the skipper had his name taken for questioning the referee. In the aftermath, Peter would assert: 'As captain of the team, I claim the right to inquire and register a protest over a decision taken by a referee'. The man in the middle thought otherwise. 'You have not lived until you have played in Welsh League football,' is what former Everton clubmate T.G. Jones told Peter upon his appointment to the Anglesey club's hot seat. Peter was mildly amused by the comment at the time, but perhaps he had cause for reflection after the incident against Pwllheli.

Certainly, the Welsh League North was no walk in the park. No concession was made by opponents for players of Peter's ability. In a match against Llandudno in January 1962, a clash of heads saw both the Holyhead skipper and Tudno's Ken Hughes hospitalised. Peter would call in on his old colleagues at Goodison Park a few days later sporting four stitches over an eye. When asked how it came about, he joked: 'From a bad pass by Jimmy Tansey.' One does wonder, with the benefit of hindsight, what role these blows to the head, with little recovery time, played in the illness Peter would live with in his final three decades. Sitting out the subsequent match against Porthmadog, the manager brought in a familiar face from his Tranmere Rovers days. Elkanah Onyeali, the Nigerian forward who had spent time at New Brighton after leaving Tranmere, responded with a debut goal and an assist.

T.G. Jones was, by now, writing a regular football column for the Welsh edition for the *Daily Post*, and took in Holyhead's Welsh Cup victory over Chester in February 1962. He used his match report to pay tribute to his former partner in the Toffees' half-back line, describing him as the inspiration for the win and 'the guiding hand which appeared to control every situation'. With a strong squad, the new manager took his club to within a point of champions Blaenau Ffestiniog in the league and secured the Alves Cup with a 6–1 rout of Colwyn Bay in the final, watched by 990 spectators. The player-manager was reported to have shown his class by pulling the strings behind the forward line.

A successful season had seen the club's revenue jump from £3,513 to £5,264 (of which £819 was gate receipts). Despite an increase in expenditure on wages and other costs, the club posted a profit of £690 and wiped away the previous debt. At the AGM, club secretary Edwin Jones attributed much of the turnaround to the player-manager: 'In his first season as player-manager with us he was a great influence on the remainder of the players who, in turn, made a wonderful endeavour to bring off the league championship.'

20
BACK HOME

It was little surprise that the manager was retained by the Anglesey club for the following season, but although he accepted, he made the decision in May to relocate his family from Birkenhead to his native Ireland. Peter would commute to Holyhead for matches by ferry from Dún Laoghaire – a significant number of Irish football supporters would take the same boat to see him in action. The crossings could be rough for manager and fans, especially during the winter months. He was quoted as saying: 'It's a big wrench to leave Merseyside after 16 years. I have enjoyed myself and made many friends here.' Before his departure, he was a guest of honour at the Everton FC Supporters' Club building, where a presentation was made in recognition of his contribution to the Blues.

The family bought a new-build semi-detached house on Beech Park Road, Foxrock, a few miles from Dalkey. At the time a semi-rural area, Foxrock has since become a prosperous outer suburb of Dublin. While the new home was constructed, the family stayed with Mabel's parents. According to Betty: 'On one side of the road were the very wealthy – on the other side were fields where they were building our house. When we started at Loreto school, they called us 'the children from the buildings', as the whole place was a building site full of semi-detached buildings that they weren't used to; they were used to huge houses with lots of land around them.'

The Farrells were not well-off when they left England – far from it, in fact. The era of the maximum wage had meant that though well paid compared to the average man in the street, there was no nest egg to see Peter and his family through his post-playing days. Whereas Tommy Eglington had his butcher's business in Clontarf to return to, which he would work in until the 1990s, Peter had no trade or pre-existing business to profit from. Fortunately, the forward-thinking Mabel had assiduously squirrelled away Peter's fees from his *Liverpool Echo* column over the years, saving enough to cover the deposit on the new house.

Mabel and Peter's fourth child, Geraldine (known by family and friends as Ger), was born in 1962, shortly after the family relocated to their homeland. The Farrell daughters remember it being a lovely place to grow up. The kids in the neighbourhood idolised Peter – he always had time for them and would go out and kick a ball with them when he came in from work and show them a few tricks. It was on one of these occasions that he was showing off some very fancy footwork when he kicked the ball into a neighbour's garden and snapped her newly planted weeping willow in half. As the lads all looked on aghast, Peter was nowhere to be seen – he had 'legged it'!

Every Thursday evening, Peter would give a series of talks on tactics and fitness and training regimes to both the senior and junior sides at Drogheda FC. He also found the time to help his local club, Dalkey United, taking a training session or two. Joe Dodd, then a player in his late teens, recalls the culture shock: 'Peter came down and took a training session in Dalkey and it was the hardest one I ever had. We just did two evenings of training a week, but he had us running and sprinting, it was the first time I felt what it was like to be really training.' Some years later, Dodd was the recipient of an award, presented by the former Ireland skipper: 'I had the privilege, when playing senior football for St Joseph's in Leinster Senior League, of getting the Player of the Year trophy from Peter at Dún Laoghaire Town Hall. Peter loved going as they had lovely cakes after it!'

Perhaps the manager being based in Ireland had a detrimental impact on the Anglesey club, but Peter was still rolling back the years on the pitch, through his football brain, if not his physicality. In an autumn defeat of Colwyn Bay, the *Daily Post*'s respected sportswriter Bob Whiting was effusive in his praise for the 40-year-old:

> Peter Farrell ... brought back memories of the days when he was the pride of the Emerald Isle. This was Irish sorcery near its best, for only Farrell really mastered the conditions as rain swept across the field, making it difficult to keep a footing. But the jog-trotting Farrell was everywhere. One minute he would be starting a move with a ball down the wing, then hovering in the centre circle holding the ball till the last second when its forward thrust would do most harm. Suddenly, he would appear on the left wing, completely unchallenged, with his old-fashioned long shorts flapping round

his knees to complete the picture of an old master.

Periodically the Irish press would link the former international skipper with appointments in his home country, but a more left-field story in the *Irish Times* in January 1963 suggested that the Holyhead coach was mulling over a £2,500 per annum (plus travelling expenses) offer to coach the Nigerian national team (maybe a connection made through Elkanah Onyeali). Nothing firm materialised, however.

Late in Peter's second season managing on Anglesey, speculation was rife in the North Wales press that his tenure would not be extended beyond the spring. With Holyhead carrying a relatively high wage bill, some committeemen openly questioned why the side had not reached a cup semi-final and were unhappy that the league title had not been wrapped up at an early stage, the club having led most of the way. The club secretary went as far as to use a general meeting as a platform to accuse some part-time professionals of not giving their all in matches. It was eventually announced that the position of player-manager for the 1963/64 season would be advertised. Reportedly, Peter was free to re-apply for his role, but the message was patently clear. Holyhead ended the season two points off eventual champions Borough United. And so, the player-manager signed off on his time

Peter photographed in his 1960s managerial days

in Wales with a goal on the last day of the season – a defeat of Prestatyn. Harold Bell was appointed as Peter's replacement and led the Harbourmen to the league title in 1963/64.

Days later, Peter was appointed manager of Drogheda, a Leinster Senior League team with ambitions to join the League of Ireland. This came as no huge surprise in light of Peter's existing connections there through speaking engagements. Having seemingly locked the football boots away once and for all, the former Ireland captain was tempted back onto the turf for a brief comeback in September 1963 by Drogheda chairman Charlie Walsh. The pair had been watching their side play Dundalk and got into conversation about what the side needed. Walsh expressed the urgency of getting a steadying influence on the pitch and told Peter that he was the ideal man to provide it. So, days later, the 41-year-old played at left-half for Drogheda against his former side, Sligo Rovers, in a League of Ireland Shield fixture at the Lourdes Stadium, a 6–2 win. This appears to have been his farewell appearance in competitive football – although he would occasionally appear in charity/benefit matches, as late as the 1980s.

Peter found a more enduring role in soccer management at T.E.K. United in south-west Dublin. Founded in 1946, the club took its name from a Dublin diary (Suttons T.E.K.) with which it had close ties. T.E.K. was an abbreviation of Tell El Kebir, an 1882 battle in Egypt in which the business's founder had fought. Competing in the Leinster Senior League Senior Division, the club brought Peter on board at the beginning of the 1964/65 season. The league's area included the wider Dublin area and was, effectively, the second-level league behind the League of Ireland. However, the creation of a League of Ireland B Division, just as Peter was appointed at T.E.K., pushed the Leinster Senior League Senior Division down to the status of a third-tier soccer competition in the Republic. The players being essentially amateur in status (some received a small wage), training was restricted to Tuesday and Thursday evenings, with matches played on the Sabbath.

Before an FAI Cup tie against Shelbourne that season, he was typically ebullient when speaking to the *Irish Times*: 'They are a grand bunch of lads, completely dedicated to football. If solid football and a will to win can do the trick, they have nothing to fear.' They would nearly cause an upset in the match at Dalymount: sticking to Peter's game plan, they led Shels until the 61st minute, before conceding three goals. Under Peter's guidance, the club won the FAI Intermediate Cup in 1965 and the Leinster Senior League title in 1964/65, retaining it a year later. In spite of their success and a preponderance of homegrown talent, it was one of the mysteries of local soccer that T.E.K. struggled to draw significant crowds to watch them on a consistent basis. Joe Dodd, in *Soccer in the Boro'*, drew a comparison with rivals Workmans Club, who only had to win a few matches to have supporters flocking through the gates.

It can be argued that T.E.K. were the best team outside of the League of Ireland from 1965 to 1980, and much of that was down to Peter's efforts and his input into the club. Joe Dodd put it beautifully: 'He gave back to the Boro' what the Boro' had given him: the love of the greatest game in the world and the heart to give his all.'

Brendan Caroll, a long-serving player who was joined at T.E.K. by his brothers Bernard and Cyril, recalls: 'Peter was a great man, a lovely man without a doubt. He was very wholehearted – in training he'd be there in his tracksuit running up and down and telling you what to do. The lads idolised him and he'd jokingly remind us that he had captained Everton and his country. He was always recognised, but he just kept it low.'

The reputation the club built up thanks to him, and the standards he set in management and coaching, meant that many T.E.K. players went on to have successful careers at League of Ireland clubs. The manager would pull on his connections to arrange occasional squad trips to Merseyside, to play a match against a Tranmere Rovers side and take in an Everton game. It left an indelible impression on Brendan Caroll: 'We were walking down the streets in Liverpool and people went mad about him. Everyone liked him and even old women were stopping him and going, "How are you, Peter?"'

A burgeoning reputation at T.E.K. led Peter to follow in Alex Stevenson's footsteps, by being appointed in September 1967 to manage one of Ireland's biggest clubs. St Patrick's Athletic, traditional rivals of his former club Shamrock Rovers, selected Peter to succeed Gerry Doyle, who had left the Inchicore side for Shelbourne. The incoming boss had precious little time to prepare his new charges for the league campaign and an Inter-Cities Fairs Cup tie against Girondins of Bordeaux. Unsurprisingly, the French team would run out 3–1 winners in the first leg and 9–4 victors on aggregate.

Before the end of the season Peter resigned, perhaps struggling to juggle the greater pressures of managing one of Ireland's leading clubs with his other work. He had been encouraged to enter the realm of insurance by his brother Gus, who was running a book for the Irish Life insurance company. Peter duly did the same for Royal Liver Insurance policies; effectively self-employed, he would visit customers and collect contributions to policies they held with the famous Merseyside company. His daughter Pauline believes that going from being a famous sportsperson to selling insurance door-to-door would have been tough for him – but his warm, talkative personality, coupled with being recognisable to people opening their front doors, was well-suited to getting a lot of business. One wonders how many football supporters were astonished to have an Irish sporting icon on their front step. Local resident Nuala Quirk Cannon recalls: 'When Peter would call to collect the premiums, there was never any rush on him. He would always come in for a chat.' Another stop on his round was the Devlin household, the family who had developed Peter as a player for Cabinteely United.

This grand man of Irish sport wasn't yet finished with football, however. Shortly after his spell at St Patrick's was curtailed, he returned to the warm embrace of T.E.K. Under his renewed leadership, the Reds added two Leinster Senior League titles (1968/69 and 1970/71) to those won under his stewardship in the mid-1960s.

A year after his return he signed Sandy Smith, a young right-back who would go on to gain Irish amateur international honours under the management of Mick Meagan and represent Sligo Rovers and Shamrock Rovers. Almost 60 years later, Smith's memories of Peter impact are undimmed:

> *I have never seen anyone like Peter for his enthusiasm for the game. He was a great trainer and motivator and we'd all do anything for him. No one had a bad word to say about him. I have never seen anyone like him for his enthusiasm for the game and he was held in the highest regard by the players, the committee and by George Sutton, owner of the club sponsors T.E.K. Dairy. I give Peter a huge amount of credit for developing and encouraging me as a player. He was a very, very special person in every way.*
>
> *As a manager, Peter had a natural ability to sum up a game. His half-time team talks were memorable for their insight and knowledge. He would speak to us as a group, and also individually to players if he needed to pass on specific instructions. He was great at communicating ideas; he didn't complicate things, his words were well chosen and they always motivated us.*
>
> *If we were performing badly, he would tell us, 'I could take any of you off at half-time, but I'm going to give you ten minutes to put things right.' The corrections he identified would regularly produce good results in the second half. We nearly always came good after one of his talks. Sometimes when he was giving team talks, Peter would mention Alan Ball as an all-action model of a player in his position. I saw that for myself at close quarters in a pre-season friendly when I played for Shamrock Rovers in 1971 against an Everton team containing the likes of Ball, Colin Harvey, Joe Royle, Howard Kendall, Keith Newton and Jimmy Husband.*
>
> *Peter was a winner and everyone at T.E.K. understood what he was about. When we would have five-a-side sessions at the end of training, even when Peter was in his late forties and early fifties, he wouldn't want to stop playing until his team went ahead. I was competitive by nature anyway, but I loved the example he set. I'm sure everyone at the club got the same kick out of that as I did. Peter's input to the club while I was there, and after, made those years for me and my teammates so memorable.*

A youngster coming through at T.E.K. was Pat Devlin, starting out on a career in football that continues to this day at Bray Wanderers. The emotions were clear when telling the author about his enduring connection to Peter:

> *I played a little bit under Peter before going to Shamrock Rovers. I then came back to T.E.K. just as he was packing it in. My childhood memories had been of soccer superstars like Peter, Charlie Hurley and Noel Cantwell. He was an absolute superstar and a gentleman. I always remember him with his pipe and his smile. He set a standard at T.E.K. He rarely gave out, but when he did, he got the message across and you knew you weren't doing your job. It was a tremendous bunch of players – people like Brendan Carroll, Eamon Turner, Brendan Bell and Ben Kerr. They were his men, who were respectable and held themselves well, and that was down to*

Peter. T.E.K. were the best side outside of the League of Ireland. It was totally football with Peter. You had to get the ball down and play it, there was no other way. It didn't matter if you were beaten if you played it right. 'It will come right,' he would say. And it did, most of the time!

In October 1970, the Leinster Cup quarter-final draw paired T.E.K. with their manager's former club, Drogheda, who just happened to be coached by Peter's one-time Everton clubmate Mick Meagan (who was also appointed as Ireland's first de facto national team manager, albeit with the FAI committeemen still having the final say on team selection). Peter was the one smiling at the end of a 2–1 shock victory at Tolka Park.

Finding it increasingly hard to combine his work as a football club manager with match reporting for Radio Eireann (more of which later) and operating his Royal Liver book, Peter left T.E.K. of his own volition in 1971. His immediate successor was Jack Nolan, a club stalwart who had played under Peter and been heavily influenced by him. Post-departure, Peter kept a close eye on news from the club, attended matches and tracked the fortunes of its players. He'd often catch up with the Carroll brothers for a chat outside their car repair business premises.

The building blocks Peter put in place at T.E.K. stood the club in good stead for years to come. The squad would continue to be trained to a level that was at least equal to top-tier League of Ireland teams. The club also benefitted from a relationship developed on the strength of Peter's reputation with St Joseph's Boys in Sallynoggin, one of the top three schoolboy teams of that era. It gave T.E.K. an invaluable conveyor belt of talent in the years to follow. According to Sandy Smith, the only constraint was the size of the club's Stradbrook Road ground, which precluded progression towards the top tier of Irish football.

An ongoing source of income and enjoyment for the Dalkey man was football commentary and analysis for state broadcaster Raidió Éireann (RTÉ from 1966). He drew on his great sporting knowledge and experience when covering the League of Ireland and some international matches. A natural in the role, his insight and warmth was appreciated by listeners. Most Sundays, the job would take him to football grounds the length and breadth of Ireland and he would often be accompanied by Sheila who was, at that time, a football fanatic. She recalls the rigmarole of Peter submitting his brief match summaries live on air from remote spots:

At 6pm there was 'Sports Report' – and Dad would have to come on it with his one-minute match report. We had a little Morris Minor; on the way back from the match we would have to find a layby on these small roads. He would get out this big leather suitcase which just fitted in the boot. He would put the back seat down, plug things in and put on the headphones – it was like something you'd see in a war film! Then it would be: 'And now over to Peter' and he'd go off doing his report as I sat in silence in the front: 'A great game here at Athlone ...' Then he'd take off the headphones, unplug everything, close up the case, put it back in the boot and we'd head home.

Family holidays did not take the Farrell family beyond Ireland. Peter had cousins in Skerries, a seaside resort to the north of Dublin, so for several summers he hired a house called The Wigwam there. That was about it for holidays, except a short break in Woodenbridge, Wicklow, in the 1970s. Frankly, Peter had no desire to travel far beyond the fairway of his local golf course. Mabel had more inclination to sample new places, so would go off on bridge holidays with friends in the 1970s.

21
FLYING THE FLAG FOR MERSEYSIDE

Always an Evertonian, Peter would be single-handedly responsible for turning a significant proportion of the Boro' 'Blue' over the years. He was also an honorary member, along with Tommy Eglington, of Club Everton Atha Cliath, a Dublin non-league team formed in 1971, which had a number of Irish Everton supporters involved. However, Peter's enduring love for Merseyside extended beyond Goodison Park to the whole Liverpool region and included all three of its senior football clubs. Indeed, he was delighted when England won the World Cup in 1966. With many boys and young men in the estate supporting Manchester United, there was no shortage of banter going on. If a match was on TV between United and either Liverpool or Everton, and the Mancunians won, they would be waiting for him to come outside and face their good-humoured taunts, but he would often hide inside.

On one occasion, Liverpool came out on top against the Red Devils while he was out at work, but no doubt listening on the car radio. The Farrell girls were sat at the dining table when they heard a car coming down the road, its horn sounding repeatedly. Mabel went to the front window and exclaimed 'Oh no!' as her husband got out of the car, not even bothering to put it in the driveway, and proceeded to walk up and down the street singing 'You'll Never Walk Alone' at the houses inhabited by Manchester United supporters. The daughters were swiftly dispatched to bring him inside before he elicited a physical response. He loved the Liverpool FC anthem, taken from the musical *Carousel*, and was often heard singing or humming it. When it came to his funeral arrangements in 1999, there was much debate as to whether, in light of his strong Everton connections, playing it during the service would be appropriate, but in the end a decision was taken to include it, as he would have wished.

Back and forth with Manchester United-supporting Foxrock residents aside, Peter was highly popular with local football supporters. He was full of stories of his career, which they loved to hear. Ger Keating, who was involved with junior football club Pearse Rovers, recalls Peter coming along to a presentation evening they were having in the Noggin Inn: 'He was so affable, brilliant with the kids, and recounted in full details his football career, with his stories of his time with Everton, Ireland and, of course, Shamrock Rovers. What I remember most is how kind, gentle and humble he was.'

Peter was always generous to a fault with the mementos of his time in football. After her father passed away, Sheila Farrell received a letter from a local man. He was a huge Evertonian who used to loiter near the Farrell house, hoping to catch a glimpse of Peter but not quite having the nerve to knock on the door. However, on one occasion, Peter came outside and they got chatting. The lad got on to telling him how his elderly grandmother was suffering from cold feet at night due to circulatory issues. Concerned to hear this, Peter headed inside, returning a few minutes later with a pair of thick woollen Irish international football socks – no socks were warmer. He handed them over and instructed the young man to put them on his granny's feet. Alas, the lad would confess in his letter to Sheila that the socks had become his prized possession, and the poor grandmother had never benefitted from wearing them!

In 1974, a panel of former Ireland internationals, including Noel Cantwell, Johnny Carey, Alan Kelly and Peter, were brought together by the *Sunday Independent* to vote on the best post-war FAI XI. Charlie Hurley, Johnny Giles and Tommy Eglington were unanimous choices. Only modesty prevented Carey, Kelly and Peter from voting for themselves and joining that list. The team chosen (in a 2–3–5 formation) was: Alan Kelly, Tony Dunne, Noel Cantwell, Peter Farrell, Charlie Hurley, Frank O'Farrell, Johnny Giles, Liam Whelan, Davie Walsh, Paddy Coad, Tommy Eglinton.

Billy Lord, the long-serving Shamrock Rovers trainer who had also served as Ireland's trainer when they won at Goodison Park in 1949, had his testimonial at Milltown. The Rovers team selected brought back memories of the days when 'house full' signs were put up at the entrances. Peter came on as a substitute and, reportedly, 'showed some of his Everton stye'.

Football would continue to dominate Peter's life – and by extension the family's – even if he was no longer employed in it on a day-to-day basis. Not that his sporting

The Farrell family together at Betty's wedding in 1975

interest was confined to football. When eldest daughter Betty tied the knot with Jim Lacy on 5 July 1975, it coincided with the Jimmy Connors vs Arthur Ashe Wimbledon final. Peter and a few others were glued to the TV set at the Farrell house until, finally, Peter reached for the off button and ushered everyone towards the church, fortunately it was situated just yards away. Four years later, Pauline was shocked at her father's apparent displeasure when she shared the date of her planned wedding date to Maurice Pratt. He was convinced that the day of the nuptials, 19 May 1979, would clash with the FA Cup final. She recalls, 'Dad was very angry about that! I never thought about it; we just picked a hotel and they gave us two possible dates in May and we chose the 19th.' A hurried check of the fixture list by the bride to be revealed that the big football day at Wembley would be a week prior to the big day in Foxrock – much to everyone's relief.

There would be rows in the household on a Saturday evening over the choice of television channel. Peter wanted to watch *Match of the Day*, but *The Late Show* – the RTÉ magazine programme hosted by Gay Byrne – was on at the same time and the female members of the family wanted to watch that. Initial approaches to the conundrum included a compromise, with half of each programme being viewed by the family. Ultimately, a more satisfactory solution was to install a TV in another room so that Peter could enjoy his dose of English football highlights, uninterrupted.

22

THE ONSET OF ILLNESS

Around 1973, Peter started to exhibit the first signs of memory loss. The symptoms started with minor things like forgetting where he had parked his car at work. They worsened slowly, yet inexorably. Medical science was a far cry from where it is now, and a formal diagnosis of Alzheimer's dementia would be some time coming. Until the dawn of the 1980s, those having a conversation with him about football and the old days would have had little inkling that something was amiss – his recall of his playing days and ability to recount stories was as sharp as ever. In stark contrast, his short-term memory capacity was deteriorating at pace. When providing commentary for matches on radio, he could wing it, being, in the words of his daughter, Ger, 'a great bluffer'. Much like the famous rugby league commentator Eddie Waring, he was able to mask that he was struggling for names and details. It was only at the end of the decade that knowledge of Peter's prognosis extended beyond family circles. When he was unable to continue with his insurance book business, Mabel returned to secretarial employment in order to ensure that the family income was maintained, and Ger was able to attend the same private school as her elder siblings had.

A sports shop in Dún Laoghaire did get Peter in to assist on a part-time basis. As a local sporting celebrity, he was quite a draw and was especially good with young customers who came in to buy football boots – regaling them with stories of the heavy boots that he had to wear in his playing days. However, as his memory loss became more severe, he was forgetting orders, and it was no longer practical for him to continue working there.

Life went on, of course, and Peter would spend endless hours traversing the local area on foot, always happy to engage passers-by in conversation. Pat Devlin recalls:

> *Peter walked everywhere and everyone would stop and say hello. Walking down the road, he'd see you and clap his hands and say, 'Come here, Devo; how are you doing?' If you met him there was no getting away from him. It was lovely to sit down and have a conversation. He was always wanting to give you a bit of advice and a little help. 'I watched you play. You should have done this and could have done that.' I listened as I was in awe of him. Peter and Mick Meagan were the most lovable of men, they were two beautiful people. They were really respected it; they never demanded it; it just happened because of who they were.*
>
> *He would often chat with Joe Dodd and, when asked by the local football historian if he resented the relatively paltry wages he had been paid during his playing days, displayed not a hint of bitterness. Quite the opposite, Peter told Dodd, football had enabled a boy who had lost his father in his early teens to play sport at the highest level and dine in the finest hotels in the world.*

In the spring of 1978, the Toffees were coming up short in a title race with Liverpool and eventual winners Nottingham Forest. However, much of the focus was on the Blues' striker Bob Latchford as he sought to reach the 30-league-goal mark and collect a cash prize put up by the *Daily Express*. He needed a brace to reach the target in the final match of the season, with Chelsea the visitors to Goodison Park. Sixteen-year-old Tony Corcoran, an avid Irish Evertonian, lived near Leopardstown racecourse where the legendary John' Jacobs had opened a golf centre in the middle of the racetrack. The teenager would earn cash collecting the empty baskets on the driving range, caddying on the local golf courses and playing a round whenever he got the opportunity. It was here, following Latchford's exploits from afar, that he came across another great Evertonian:

> *I would often bring my small handheld radio to my workplace at the golf centre on Saturdays, as I listened to the football scores and commentary on whatever game was featured. April the 29th, 1978, was a day when something magical was about to happen. Bob Latchford needed two goals against Chelsea to win £10,000 for reaching the total of 30 goals in a league season. Being an Everton fan was not exactly a bed of roses as the club had struggled since they last won the league in 1970. I knew of a few Everton fans locally, but my world was about to change that afternoon.*

THE LIFE AND TIMES OF PETER FARRELL

Although not quite reaching the level of Tommy Eglington, Peter enjoyed his golf. He was also adept at tennis, swimming and table tennis

I had made sure I was ahead of my work and had positioned myself in the last bay at the very end of the outdoor driving range for the 3pm kick-off. I had my bucket of golf balls ready to hit out and my radio tuned in as the sun shone and the referee's whistle blew. Everton were well up for this game and by half time it was 2–0 – but no goals for our Big Bob. The driving range was filling up and I heard a few murmurs of disgruntled golfers wondering why this kid was listening to a crackling radio football commentary as he hit golf balls. I heard later that there were a few complaints in the shop, but the staff knew me and just ignored them.

The second half kicked off and Neil Robinson made it 3–0. Cue another goal celebration from me and raised eyebrows from the golfers. It was then that this man moved from six bays up to the bay beside me. I expected the worst and was waiting to be told to turn that radio off ... but nothing happened as he just went about practising his shots. Mick Buckley puts in a cross and Latch scores. My reaction was to jump around as if I had scored it myself and next thing I know, my new neighbour is joining in! He had moved down to listen to the match and here we were forgetting all about the golf as he introduced himself as another Everton fan.

Next up Mick Lyons makes it 5–0 and still Bob needed one more goal to win the big prize. The tension was mounting and suddenly Everton have a penalty. There was only one man for the job as Latchford stepped up and scores to take his tally to 30 goals and win the prize. Here in Dublin two strangers celebrated as if they had scored, whilst a host of golfers looked on bemused by the carry-on. That stranger then introduced himself as Peter Farrell and told me he once played for Everton. I didn't recognise him but knew the name immediately, as Peter Farrell was an Everton and Ireland legend. Peter was a regular at the driving range and would happily spend hours practising his game.

Peter loved his golf and, of course, Everton. Stories were told and retold over that summer and my desire to see Everton at Goodison was realised in October as I made it to the 'Andy King' Merseyside derby. What a first match to go to, and to top it off, we went down to the old supporters' club near Goodison after the game. Not being members, we were stopped at the door by a gentleman with army medals on his jacket. He was quick enough to spot the Dublin accents and welcomed us like long-lost brothers as he brought us down the corridor to show us an Irish international football cap belonging to none other than my new pal Peter Farrell.

Peter's role in providing some of the best football seen at Prenton Park was not forgotten on the Wirral. In 1971, he had been accompanied by Tommy Eglington and fellow notable Irish players Noel Kelly and Peter Doherty to a sportsman's dinner held at the Birkenhead club. Nine years later, Tommy and Peter were, once again, esteemed guests at an event held at the stadium to mark the 25th anniversary of the founding of the Tranmere Rovers Supporters' Association. Peter would later recall being made an honorary life vice-president of the club, musing mirthfully, 'For someone who had been sacked with two years left of a managerial contract to run, it was an amusing turnaround.' With Rovers struggling badly in the 1980s, one supporter recalled that Peter held the honorary role and wrote to him, stating – perhaps in jest – that this was having a detrimental impact on the club and that he might consider resigning! Peter put it down to Merseyside wit!

Tommy Eglington, Liverpool FC Secretary Peter Robinson, Con Martin and Peter Farrell on Merseyside circa 1980

Having reminisced at the Prenton Park event about their time with Rovers, the pair caught up over a few drinks in the subsequent days with Harry Leyland, the one-time Everton and Tranmere goalkeeper who was, by this time, running a market stall in Birkenhead.

With Everton playing away that Saturday, the former Toffees heroes were at a loose end, so Tommy put a call in to Anfield to see if they might be able to get seats for the Liverpool match. On giving his name, the former Blues' winger was asked, 'You're still alive, are you?!' Once it had been firmly established that the pair were hale and hearty, arrangements were put in place. On arriving at Anfield, the Reds' former rivals were shown to seats in the directors' box and treated as honoured guests. Bob Paisley, the Liverpool manager who had broken Blue hearts in the 1950 FA Cup semi-final, got word to the pair that he would meet them after the match for a catch-up. Even the groundsman called by for a chat. Peter told the *Liverpool Echo*: 'Tommy and I had a wonderful day. There are very few clubs who would take in two old players from another club – and great rivals, at that – and welcome them so generously.'

Of course, Peter and Tommy were never forgotten by the Reds' rivals and were present at the Everton centenary event held at the Littlewood's JM Building in the autumn of 1978. Joining them were the likes of Alex Stevenson and Ted Sagar.

That same year, Peter gave an interview to a *Liverpool Echo* journalist. As well as indicating that he was committing his career memories to paper (sadly, no such notes have been located), he gave his theories about what makes a good manager: 'Everyone believes good players automatically make good managers, but that's a load of rubbish.' He elaborated by naming former Everton clubmates Harry Catterick and Ron Saunders as two footballers with modest playing careers who enjoyed success from the dugout. As a counterpoint he cited Peter Doherty and Johnny Carey, 'football gods' in his words, as wonderful players who lacked the ability, when managers, to get their message through to their players. One compatriot he felt did have the 'indefinable thing in his character' was John Giles, who, he said, commanded respect and had an aura of confidence.

In 1984, Peter's daughter Pauline and two sons-in-law (acting as 'minders' in light of his dementia) took him to Wembley for the League Cup Final – the first time that Everton and Liverpool had come up against each other in the final of a major competition. The highlight of the day for Peter was not the hard-fought goalless draw, but coming across a small stallholder on Wembley Way selling vintage football cigarette cards. While rooting through them he came across one depicting himself. He said to the seller, 'Do you know who this is?' The seller replied: 'Some old fella who played for Everton years ago.' Thrilled with his find, he purchased the card and brought it home to Foxrock.

The following autumn, Everton were drawn against University College Dublin (UCD) in the European Cup Winners' Cup. Evertonian Jimmy Brown had travelled over with family and friends from Fazakerley on Merseyside for the match – Everton's first in a European competition since 1979. The night before the match, he was in a central Dublin bar, engaging the landlord in conversation, when the publican pointed to an older gentleman sat quietly in the corner with a friend or family member and informed Brown that this was Peter Farrell, former Everton skipper. He promptly brought Peter and his companion into the conversation and listened, enraptured, to the tales of his playing career. Needless to say, Peter never had to buy a drink that evening. Peter and Tommy Eglington attended the match – readily mixing with UCD and Everton supporters.

As his attention span diminished, the family thought it best that he did not regularly attend matches after this; the TV, with the football on, would be on at home, and he could dip in and out of it as the mood took him.

A familiar figure in and around the Foxrock, Dún Laoghaire and Dalkey areas, Peter was always happy to engage with friends and strangers that he met when out and about. On Sundays, he might go to a League of Ireland match or a junior fixture in his locality. If that proved unexciting, he would venture on to another match or, sometimes, take a stroll down to the waterfront. Even 25 years after his passing, Peter is fondly remembered in the area – as evidenced when the author put out an appeal for memories of the former football star. A small sample is included here:

My dad was from Sandycove. He told me that he was an altar boy at Peter's wedding. Dad was an Everton fan because of Peter. We grew up on Clonkeen Road and Dad met Peter when he lived in Foxrock. I grew up with stories about Peter, especially when he played for the Irish team that beat England, that they never acknowledged. I remember the sports shop Peter worked at in Dún Laoghaire. I met him a few times when I was a kid; he was a lovely man.

Jimmy Byrden

My memory of him locally was when he played tennis in Sandycove Tennis Club. None of us believed he'd had such a great career until he brought down stuff from his playing career the following week! An absolute legend.

Ger FitzGerald

23
THE LONG FAREWELL

In a fitting effort to recognise those who had made a considerable contribution to Irish soccer, Peter became the second person, after Joe Haverty, to be made a guest of honour of the FAI at an international match. It was when Uruguay came to Lansdowne Road for a friendly match in April 1986, an appropriate choice as Peter had been in the side the first time Ireland had taken on South American opponents (Argentina) in May 1951. After lunch in a Dublin hotel, Peter and his family were to be given VIP treatment at the stadium. Sheila Farrell picks up the poignant story of the afternoon:

> *So, Mum, Dad, his brother Jim and I went. At half-time, over the loudspeaker they started speaking about Dad and his career and then a guy asked Peter to go down to the pitch with him. We didn't expect any of this. They brought him to the middle of the pitch and the whole crowd stood up! Everybody stood up and gave him an ovation. We were gobsmacked that, in spite of his Alzheimer's, it seemed to all come back to him and he waved to the crowd. God, that was his whole life when he was younger, playing in front of those crowds. RTÉ was waiting to interview him, and Mum was worried that she had put him in his old overcoat — as you don't wear your best clothes*

to a match and she had no idea this was going to happen. When Dad came back into his seat, I said, 'Dad, that was amazing!' and he replied, 'Yes, very nice, very nice,' and some tears rolled down his cheeks. It was one of those really sad moments. It had all come back as he stood in the middle of Lansdowne Road as they interviewed him about 1949 – but a few minutes later he would not have remembered my name.

At this point in time, Jack Charlton was moulding the Irish national team, bolstering it with footballers from England, Scotland and Wales with Irish roots. This transformative work culminated in qualification for the 1988 European Championship finals, followed by the 1990 and 1994 World Cup finals. The family were upset that Peter, due to his illness, never got to fully appreciate the joy of the side's success over that period; it was something that would have filled him with immense pride.

In May 1987, with Shamrock Rovers on the point of leaving their home stadium at Milltown, Peter lined up in a Hoops 'golden oldies' team also containing Paddy Coad, Eamonn Darcy and Liam Tuohy competing in a 60-minute charity match – perhaps the last time he laced up his football boots.

He gave an interview for the Everton matchday programme's Goodison Greats feature in March 1991, photographed proudly holding the silver Shamrock awarded to him by the FAI. He spoke of his pride at playing for two great football clubs in Shamrock Rovers and Everton. He had recently watched the epic FA Cup tie between the Toffees and Liverpool which needed two replays to settle it in the Blues' favour. He confessed to this bringing him thorough enjoyment, but he conceded that he had not relished playing in matches against the Reds: 'Merseyside derbies were great to watch,

The former Ireland skipper photographed in 1991, proudly holding the silver shamrock awarded for 25 appearances for the FAI Ireland team (credit: Everton FC)

but terrible to play in. There was too much at stake.' He went on to confirm that he was still in love with the game, and would watch quite a lot of local junior football, knowing that if a match was not proving entertaining, he could just walk away.

In the mid-1990s, Peter's dementia had advanced to the point where he would frequently go AWOL, causing great angst until he could be located and brought home by family members or friendly local residents. The illness also led to distressing changes in his demeanour – this once warm, avuncular man would have bouts of anger. Sandy Smith, his former T.E.K. player and golf partner, recalled: 'I found it particularly tough to see when he struggled to remember things and, out of his normal character, got annoyed – which wasn't his fault, at all.'

The grandson of Christy Devlin, Peter's manager at Cabinteely, also called Christy Devlin, had been a League of Ireland footballer but also worked in a taxi business. In the 1990s he had a surprise encounter with Peter, who he'd remembered as the cheerful man calling at his door to collect the Royal Liver premiums: 'We had a contract with the Eastern Health Board – one night I got a call to pick someone up from hospital. I got the man into the car, his hands were bandaged. When we arrived at the destination, I got out of the car to get my docket and asked him to wait inside; it was only then that I realised it was Peter.'

In 1993, after much soul-searching, the family concluded that this much-loved man required residential care. A suitable facility, Vergemount Clinic in Clonskeagh Hospital, was carefully chosen and Peter moved on a Friday afternoon. Come the following Sunday, the family received the news that its newest resident had gone missing, having failed to attend the local church service. A morning of increasingly fraught searching ensued, with the Farrells enlisting the help of all and sundry. The task was made all the more difficult by a women's mini-marathon being staged in the area, with motor traffic barred from numerous roads. To the relief of all, the 'escapee' was located at the finish line of the race, having become the only (unofficial) male entrant. It transpired that, stumbling on the event on the way to the church, he had jogged – wearing his Sunday best – alongside the participants, encouraging them and coaching them along the way! Safely ensconced back at the care home, red in the face from his exertions and crimson of scalp from sunburn, he told his daughter Ger that it had been 'quite the morning'.

Several more 'breakouts' occurred. Local public transport was Peter's favoured method of traversing the Dublin suburbs. Once he ended up in Crumlin – a nurse on a bus saw him sitting on a bench and, recognising him, got the word back to the family and care home so that he could be retrieved. The question asked was how he was achieving these Houdini-esque feats. It was eventually established that his method of escape was brilliantly simple. If a visitor was leaving the institution, as they went through the door, he would call out, 'Just hold the door, please.' Not realising that the smartly dressed man coming along behind them was a resident, they would oblige, and within seconds he would be free to roam.

Another mirthful, if bittersweet, moment thrown up by the terrible disease occurred at a golf driving range. Mick Meagan had been a fine, loyal friend to his former Everton clubmate during his long illness, regularly taking him for trips out from the care home. Not one to seek attention or praise, Meagan had not even told Peter's family that he was doing these good deeds – they only discovered some time later. As the pair hit a few golf balls at the range, Peter suddenly decided that he was going to collect those balls already hit from the bays. Off he headed with a bucket, directly into the line of fire from other golfers. Meagan hot-footed it after him and successfully returned his former club captain to the safety of a bay before any harm could be done. Two watching golfers informed the chaperone that it was just as well it was Peter Farrell, and not Tommy Eglington, that he was chasing. The reason? He would never have caught up with 'Eggo', the former flying winger!

Although there were moments of humour, seeing such a warm, intelligent and gregarious personality recede into the miasma of dementia was extremely difficult for his nearest and dearest. In 1994, his immense contribution to Irish soccer was recognised with his induction into the FAI Hall of Fame – it was a shame that it could not have come sooner, when he would have been able to appreciate the recognition. Although he was long past being able to attend football matches, Everton kindly saw to it that two of his daughters had tickets for Everton's FA Cup final victory over Manchester United in 1995.

Some of his old T.E.K. comrades would take the trouble to visit Peter, including Pat Devlin:

> *My relationship with him was unbelievable, right up to the last. We never forgot him. Three or four of us would go and see him in the home twice a month, nobody would make a big deal of it. We would sit down and talk about football and then he'd say, 'You lads had better go, you'll be late for training.' I have been fortunate to have a reasonable career in soccer – but it was paved by people like Peter and Mick Meagan. I never hit the heights that Peter did, but I was so happy to have known him, he was an absolute superstar. I can still see the big smile on his face.*

News broke on 16 March 1999 that this grand man of Irish sport had passed away at the age of 76. Although his health had been failing, the passing came sooner than had been anticipated by his loved ones. The funeral Mass was held at the nearby Church of Our Lady of Perpetual Succour on 18 March. As previously mentioned, 'You'll Never Walk Alone' got an airing, which may have confused some Evertonians in the congregation. The recessional hymn was 'Abide With Me', one so closely associated with football.

Tributes poured in from Merseyside and across Ireland. Irish newspapers gave appropriate prominence to a figure who had, in the words of journalist Peter Byrne, been 'a model sportsman, an inspiring captain, a superbly dedicated club man'. Byrne finished his tribute by stating, succinctly, 'He adorned Irish football.'

The subsequent Everton matchday programme featured an extensive item on the club's late captain. It included a heartfelt tribute from Dave Hickson, who had benefitted from Peter's sage advice, and letters from supporters who had idolised him. Ron Tennant, who had first seen Peter play in 1947, wrote: 'I could go on and on about the virtues of Peter Farrell. He played football for Everton like it should be played: full of enthusiasm and pride in the blue shirt.'

Mabel, Sheila and Ger visited Merseyside in December 2002, visiting the former family homes in Bootle and Birkenhead – an opportunity for Mabel to renew the acquaintance of old friends. Sheila and Ger attended Goodison Park to watch the Toffees take on Blackburn Rovers. Fittingly, an Irish international midfielder, Lee

Mabel Farrell at the opening of her late husband's alcove at the FAI headquarters in 2011

Carsley, was on the scoresheet in a 2–1 win. The previous day, the sisters were treated to a tour of the stadium by Peter's former teammate Dave Hickson, who regaled them with stories of their time together. He joked that Peter and Mabel had been the 'Posh and Becks' of the mid-1950s.

In 2001 Dalkey United commissioned sculptor Paul Ferriter to produce bronze busts to celebrate the area's two finest footballing sons, Paul McGrath and Peter Farrell. It was unveiled in the presence of his wife, family and some former teammates. On the night of their official unveiling at the club, McGrath was there, along with members of the Farrell family. The former, who had played for Dalkey as a youth, had a lovely chat with Pauline's sons. A decade later, Peter was honoured posthumously at the FAI head office with the creation of an 'alcove' tribute gallery, featuring memorabilia from his illustrious career. This is a status shared with a select few others, including Liam Tuohy, Mick Meagan and Noel Cantwell.

Peter and Mabel's daughters pay a final visit to Goodison Park in 2025

Although Peter had no sons, there are eight grandsons and a granddaughter. The sporting gene has certainly been passed down. The eldest of Pauline's five sons, Alan, was regularly watched by his grandmother Mabel when coming through as a soccer player with St Joseph's Boys. He had two spells with Wayside Celtic of the Leinster Senior League, sandwiching a period playing in Australia. Second son Rory moved from Bray Wanderers Under-21 side to have a soccer scholarship at the University of Mary, North Dakota. Third-born son Stephen also headed to the USA, with scholarships in Flagler College and Florida Southern. Gary was less sporting inclined, but shone academically, while the youngest, Niall, headed to West Texas on a golf scholarship and now lives in Hong Kong. Betty's three sons, Nat, Ronan and David, played rugby, tennis and Gaelic football in their youth but did not pursue them to a high level, while their sister, Fiona, played hockey.

Mabel Carney, who gladly sacrificed so much to support her husband and family through the good years and the difficult times of Peter's illness, passed away on 19 April 2017. A loving wife, mother, grandmother and great-grandmother, she was laid to rest, reunited with her beloved husband, in Deansgrange Cemetery.

With Goodison Park entering its final months before Everton's move to a gleaming new stadium on the waterfront, Peter and Mabel's four daughters made an emotional last visit to Goodison in February 2025. They were treated to a behind the scenes tour, resisting the temptation to recreate their father's famous goal for Ireland at the Gwladys Street End. The following day they watched the Toffees take on Manchester United. Time was also found to visit the Bridewell pub and raise a glass to its former occupant, their great-grandfather James Farrell, and give thanks that John Hayes' revolver failed to function in 1891.

POSTSCRIPT

When a panel was assembled late in 1999 to select an 'Everton Giant' for each decade of the 20th century, it was Dave Hickson, the talismanic, buccaneering blond-haired striker, who got the vote for the 1950s, with the immaculate T.G. Jones getting the nod for the decade prior. Peter was shortlisted for the 1950s but Hickson was the overwhelming choice. So, where does Peter Farrell sit in the pantheon of Everton and Irish footballers and captains?

The case for his status is hampered by it being six decades since his salad days in the blue and green shirts of club and country, respectively. First-hand testimony of him as a footballer is becoming scarce and match footage featuring the wing-half, is frustratingly fleeting, making it even harder to make a fair assessment.

The pages of this biography have explored the qualities of the Dalkey man, on and off the pitch. He was genial, a great enthusiast for his chosen sport and a fierce yet fair competitor. Never a virtuoso, he was a players' player and a dream to manage, as evidenced by Cliff Britton selecting him as his Everton captain through all but one of his season's at the helm. It was a wise choice. Through his personality, infectious enthusiasm and unstinting effort in the blue shirt – rather than being from the ranting school of captaincy – Peter was a superb leader of men in often tough times at

Goodison Park. A sentence written at the time of his departure from the Toffees neatly sums up his influence of the team: 'Peter is always to be found where the action is thickest, urging his team to greater effort.' Jack Taylor, Dixie Dean, Jock Thomson, Roy Vernon, Brian Labone, Kevin Ratcliffe and Dave Watson may have got their hands on trophies, but Mike Lyons, Séamus Coleman and Peter rank alongside them as some of the finest to lead Everton sides across the touchline.

For Ireland, his achievements may have been eclipsed by the glory years of the late 1980s and early 1990s under Jack Charlton, yet here was a player handed the captaincy on his international debut and who was just the second to receive the highly prized silver shamrock to mark 25 appearances for his country. John Giles, in his 2010 memoir *A Football Man – The Heart of the Game* listed the five traits that, in his view, made a great team player. They are:

> *1. Whatever the abilities the player possesses must be used for the benefit of the team. This requires honesty of effort.*
>
> *2. Moral courage is needed to take responsibility in accepting the ball, no matter how important the game and regardless of the score.*
>
> *3. An honest effort must be made to regain possession when the other team has the ball.*
>
> *4. There must be no public remonstration with teammates.*
>
> *5. A player must have the intelligence and humility to play the simple pass when that is the right thing to do.*

These five characteristics sum up Giles' predecessor in the Ireland team to a tee. Talented, hardworking and selfless in supporting the team's cause.

Above all else, Peter Farrell was a great family man who, supported by his loving family, lived stoically with advancing dementia, which came far too early in his 76 years.

It is fitting to end with Peter's words of advice to anyone hoping to make their way in football, counsel which is as relevant now as it was when he gave it many decades ago:

> *Train hard, make sure you always place your team before your own personal success and glory. And above all, take good care you don't get a swelled head. I can assure you, if you play every game with these objects in mind, although you may never become a star, you will derive utmost satisfaction from each and every game knowing that, although you may not have played well, you played the game by doing your best.*

THE LIFE AND TIMES OF PETER FARRELL

Peter Desmond Farrell - the Emerald Evertonian

TOMMY EGLINGTON
THE FLYING WINGER
OF THE 1950S

It would be remiss to produce a biography of Peter Farrell without giving his dear friend and teammate Tommy Eglington a share of the spotlight. This chapter attempts to do that.

Tommy was born in Donnycarney, a Northside suburb of Dublin, on 15 January 1923. He was one of seven siblings born to butcher Christopher Eglington and his wife Margaret. As was the norm, Gaelic football was played in school, so Tommy would only get to indulge his passion for the 'British game' in the fields near his home after school lessons had finished. His early footballing experience was with Grace Park, a Sunday team he formed with friends (it disbanded when the war broke out). While on a tour of the English Midlands with Grace Park he was offered a trial with West Bromwich Albion but he turned it down, feeling that he was too young to leave home. Tommy went on to play for Munster Victoria and Distillery before being picked up by Southside club Shamrock Rovers in the early 1940s. Joining Peter Farrell there, the left-winger appeared in three successive FAI Cup finals.

Away from football Tommy worked in the family butchery firm, alongside his father and three brothers (he also had two sisters).

As is detailed in the main body of this book, Tommy and Peter were spotted by

Tommy proudly wearing his Ireland shirt in the mid-1940s

Everton's secretary-manager Theo Kelly and chairman Ernest Green when Shamrock Rovers played Glentoran in Belfast in 1946. It set in chain negotiations which culminated in the Rovers pair joining the Toffees in mid-July. This came after Tommy had debuted for Ireland (FAI) alongside Peter in Portugal.

Within a couple of days of disembarking in Liverpool, the Irishmen had been placed by their new employer in digs with the Egan family in Bootle. The kind-hearted landlady became like a second mother to the pair and helped them settle on Merseyside. Tommy recalled a decade later: 'We never felt a moment's strangeness or anxiety. Right from the start we were made to feel as though we "belonged" and that we were one of the family. I shall never forget the happy days I spent in Harris Drive.'

Tommy made a brilliant debut for the reserves in a Central League fixture at Hillsborough. He progressed to the first team at Goodison on 11 September – replacing the veteran Wally Boyes in the number 11 shirt for the visit of Arsenal. The result was a morale-boosting 3–2 victory. Stork wrote in the *Daily Post* that Tommy had 'a successful debut without pulling up trees'. One pleasing aspect was the quick understanding established on the left of attack with compatriot Alex Stevenson. One match report noted: 'Changes had to be made, and these undoubtedly were all to the good. Don't think that all is well, but there was definitely more combination in the side. Stevenson's return to link up with the new Irish laddie, Eglington, was a happy stroke, for Wee Alec holds the ball, he slips it out to the open spaces and if his colleagues sense what he is about they move into those spaces.'

Later that month Tommy lined up with Stevenson, who was recalled after a long absence due to the unavailability of a number of Northern Irish players, in the green shirt of Ireland (FAI) for the first visit of the England team to Dublin since 1912. Peter Farrell missed out as he was unavailable through injury. The fixture was the result of an approach by the FAI to the English FA, inviting them to send a team to mark the golden jubilee of the Dublin-based organisation. The offer was accepted on condition of the provision of good accommodation and catering plus an acceptable financial package (their half-share of gate receipts would amount to £3,557). President Seán T. O'Kelly attended the match, played on 30 September, and saw Tommy have a fine match but, with nine minutes left on the clock, Tom Finney grabbed the solitary goal to secure a hard-fought win for the visitors.

Tommy was joined in the Everton team in late November by his former Shamrock Rovers clubmate, now recovered from his ankle injury, and they were practically inseparable in the side for the decade to come. Tommy got off the mark in his sixth appearance for the Blues. It was very welcome as the Toffees had not scored in the previous 298 minutes of play – an indication of the struggles being experienced. However, the goal came in a 4–1 pummelling at Roker Park. Aside from briefly losing his place to Boyes over the festive period, Tommy became the go-to man for the number 11 jersey for almost the entire duration of his stay at Everton.

Five months after his FAI Ireland debut, the winger was called up in November 1946 for the first of six appearances for the Belfast-based IFA Ireland side. He lined up with Peter Farrell, Alex Stevenson and Johnny Carey in a goalless draw with Scotland and a year later featured in a stirring 2–2 draw with England at Goodison Park. This would be one of his greatest performances on his home club's turf. The watching Ranger stated that Tommy provided 'brilliant fireworks' on this 5 November fixture, adding: 'Tommy, that day, had everything it takes – speed, ball control and a trickiness which had Laurie Scott, England's right-back, running around in circles

Tommy signing a visitors book in the mid-1950s, watched by dignitaries and Alex Stevenson (Ireland coach and Tommy's former Everton clubmate) watching on (credit: Eglinton family)

like a dog trying to catch his own tail.'

From 1948 onwards his appearances would solely be for the FAI – his 24th and last being in a fixture with Spain in November 1955. In that era clubs were not obligated to release their players for international fixtures, but Tommy would recall that Everton respected his patriotic desires: 'They always treated me fairly when international honours came my way. There was never any moaning about the loss of services for a club game. It is things such as these which give players a feeling for a club.'

One of the biggest regrets in his long football career was not being selected for the Irish side to face England at Goodison Park on 21 September 1949. Tommy O'Connor of Shamrock Rovers got the nod to play, with suspicions that the choice made was connected to placing O'Connor in the 'shop window'. Tommy watched from the stand as Ireland, with clubmates Peter Farrell and Peter Corr in green shirts, inflicted the first defeat on England on home soil by a non-British team.

Determined to make the most of his natural assets and continually improve, Tommy led a healthy lifestyle and was a dedicated trainer. With that and the luck of avoiding serious injury – maybe defenders could not get near enough to clobber him

THE EMERALD EVERTONIAN

Tommy and his Everton teammates are introduced to British Prime Minister Clement Atlee by club captain Peter Farrell

The Toffees card school not long after Tommy and Peter joined the club. They are up against Wally Fielding and Ted Sagar

Tommy attacks the Park End goal as Everton teammate Harry Catterick watches on

– it is little wonder that he enjoyed a long career. Supporters accustomed to being enraptured by the flair and trickery of Jack Coulter and Wally Boyes on the Everton left flank before the war now embraced a winger who would dispense with frippery and rely on blistering pace to leave right-backs trailing in his wake. His was a direct, barnstorming style of wing play which soon won admirers on the terraces. Affectionately known as 'Flash Eggo' in recognition of his jet-heeled properties, Tommy was described thus by Everton teammate (and subsequently trainer) Gordon Watson: 'Tommy had the fastest feet in the game and Theo Kelly often joked that he'd received a complaint from fans in the Paddock about the smell of scorched turf.' Mick Meagan, who joined the club six years after his countryman, recalled: 'When an Aer Lingus plane flew over Goodison we'd say, "There's Eggo flying up the wing!"'

Stepping up to the top flight of English football was not seamless, and Tommy's play had rough edges. In an honest critique published in 1949, the journalist Ranger acknowledged that Tommy could give the best full-backs the run-around on his day, but could be inconsistent with his wing play and erratic with his shooting. Much of

Training with Peter on the pitchside track, both Irishman took maintaining their fitness very seriously

this he put down to an 'impetuous and temperamental' streak which was probably the result of an intense eagerness to do well for the team. It was suggested that, to improve, he should try 'a little less hard'. Ranger also highlighted that the right foot of the naturally left-sided forward left much to be desired (a comment often made about Dwight McNeil, who played in a similar role for the Blues nearly seven decades later). Certainly, Tommy became a more polished, less impetuous player with experience, and worked hard on his right-foot kicking. By the early 1950s, he was willing and able to cut inside and have a crack at goal with his 'swinger' – with a number of his 82 goals for the club coming from that source.

Back home in Ireland, Tommy married Doris 'Dorrie' O'Donohue – a cashier in a grocery establishment – in the summer of 1950. There are no prizes for guessing that the best man was Peter Farrell. On returning to Liverpool, the newlyweds lodged for several months with Tommy's landlady Mrs Egan on Harris Lane in Bootle until moving into a club house on Mostyn Avenue in Old Roan. Dorrie had been filled with trepidation at moving from her homeland, much as Tommy had felt in 1946. 'I need not have worried,' she told the *Liverpool Echo* a few years later. 'Right from the start I found a warm and sincere welcome which could not have been more genuine if I had been starting my married life in Dublin.'

In Old Roan, the Eglingtons found another extremely friendly community which embraced them. It prompted Tommy to state, 'Like my clubmate, I reckon that Liverpool folk are the warmest-hearted in the country. And I don't think that just springs from the fact that we are professional footballers, but from the natural kindness of the folk themselves. They are built that way.' The couple, who raised three children, Anthony, Bernard and Paula, became members of the congregation at the nearby Holy Rosary Church. The arrival of Anthony and Bernard restricted Dorrie's opportunities to watch her husband don the royal blue shirt. Aside from domestic chores she would enjoy knitting, reading and watching some evening television – she would admit to regretting being unable to Goodison Park often.

It was Tommy's misfortune that his best years were spent in the doldrums of the Second Division, having endured the ignominy of relegation in 1951 (ironically, it was his most prolific scoring season to date, with eight league goals). His greatest feat in the royal blue shirt occurred on 27 September 1952 when he scored five goals in a 7–1 rout of Doncaster Rovers (player-managed by his friend, the Ireland star Peter Doherty). Tommy, looking back some years later, said, 'I remember two headers the most vividly. Both crosses from the right wing and I met them at the far post and nodded them in.' Smiling, he noted that he had not been too greedy as John Willie Parker also weighed in with two goals! Although he cherished the memory for the rest of his life, he had no physical memento of the match: 'It was a great day for me, but I didn't get the ball to keep. It wasn't done in those days.'

His impressive haul had journalists leafing through the record books to check for precedents. Dixie Dean had scored five for the Toffees on three occasions, while

Jack Southworth went one better when knocking six past the West Bromwich Albion goalkeeper in 1893. Both were, of course, great centre-forwards rather than wide men. Ranger, in the *Liverpool Echo*, wrote: 'Eglington has written his name in football annals in a manner that dozens of outstanding wingers of former days never achieved.' It had been 32 years since an Irishman – Brighton and Hove Albion's Jack Doran – had achieved the same scoring feat in a Football League match.

The Dubliner missed only one match in the 1953/54 season as Everton earned promotion back to the top-flight. In fact, he never made fewer than 30 appearances in all but his last season at the club – a remarkable record, comparable to that of Peter Farrell. He viewed the promotion season as a highlight of his career and recalled the journey to the final game of the season at Boundary Park: 'Apart from the result, my outstanding memory was the support we had that night. We travelled along the East Lancs Road and it was packed with Everton supporters waving blue and white favours and cheering us on. It was an amazing sight.'

Tommy married Dorrie O'Donohue in 1950. Unsurprisingly he chose Peter Farrell to be his best man

He reached the 350 league matches appearance mark in December 1955, but the arrival of head coach Ian Buchan in 1956 marked a shift towards blooding younger players. It followed that Tommy's days in the Blues' number 11 shirt were numbered, even though he could still show a clean pair of heels to many a full-back. One of the emerging local players in the mid-1950s was Brian Harris, who later told the Everton matchday programme: 'When I got into the first team I was well looked after by Eggo and all these players. When you are a young player that helps you a hell of a lot because they know how things work; they passed everything they learnt to me. Eggo was a good player, very quick. I can't say enough about him. He was a smashing guy; we had a lot of laughs and he'd always help you if you had any problems.'

THE EMERALD EVERTONIAN

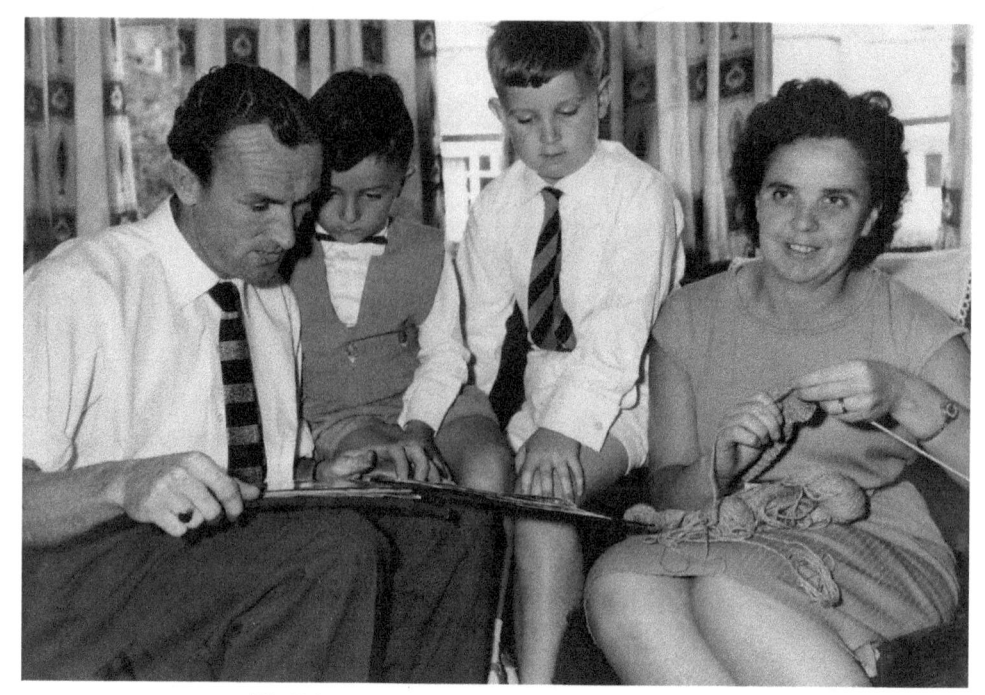

The Eglington family at home in Liverpool in the mid-1950s

Everton's Irish trio of Peter Farrell, Jimmy O'Neill and Tommy Eglington on board the MV Munster at Dublin in October 1953

THE LIFE AND TIMES OF PETER FARRELL

The Everton team at an away fixture in the early 1950s

Tommy needs all of his trademark pace to avoid getting mobbed by enthusiastic Evertonians

Welshman Graham Williams took Tommy's place on the left wing towards the end of the 1956/57 season. The 34-year-old's final Everton Football League appearance came in a home defeat to Portsmouth on 23 March 1957, but he bowed out in fitting fashion in May when Everton played Shamrock Rovers in Dublin (for the record, Rovers won 4–2). A month previously, his was one of a number of names

The Toffees on a beach, only Tommy and Peter wear their club blazers

announced as being open to transfer by the Toffees. In late June of that year the Merseyside press picked up on efforts being made by Third Division Tranmere Rovers to acquire the left-winger's services and a £1,750 deal was swiftly finalised. Ranger, writing in the *Liverpool Echo*, lamented Tommy's departure from Goodison Park, while recognising that time waits for no man:

> *We shall miss Eglington at Goodison Park – and possibly in more ways than one. I had hoped the same clemency might be extended to Eglington, bearing in mind his eleven years of whole-hearted service to the club and the fact that never once had he caused them a moment's anxiety. Fortunately, he has got fixed up all right. Eglington might not always have been everyone's idea of a first-class winger. He had spells when he suffered off periods. But so does every player. Taken by and large over the eleven years, however, he gave Everton good value for his wages and missed barely a couple of dozen matches.*
>
> *Football today is very strictly business – there is little or no room for sentiment. Nevertheless, it is still a matter for regret when time brings its inevitable changes and*

Firm friends since 1943, Peter and Tommy spending time together in the 1980s

a noted player has to step down into a lower sphere where the cheers of the smaller crowds make less sweet music than those to which he has so long been accustomed.

At the time of crossing the Mersey to the Wirral, Tommy had amassed 428 appearances for the Blues. This makes him, as at September 2025, the 13th-highest appearance-maker, just behind compatriot Séamus Coleman. Everton did not find a satisfactory long-term successor for the number 11 shirt for over half a decade. Tommy Ring, a Scot with Irish ancestry, had dazzled on the left wing in 1960 before suffering a badly broken leg. John Morrissey's arrival from Liverpool in 1962 finally brought the Blues' long search to an end.

Soon joined at Prenton Park by Peter Farrell, Tommy enjoyed four productive seasons as a Rover. He was almost an ever-present and racked up 185 appearances in league and cups. In spite of sustaining a fractured fibula in April 1960, he was back fit for the 1960/61 season. On 17 April 1961 he bowed out from competitive football in this land – as fate would have it, it was at Goodison Park in the Liverpool Senior Cup semi-final. Watching the 4–1 victory for the Toffees from the stands was Tommy's ex-strike partner, Harry Catterick, who had been appointed to the post of Everton manager earlier that day. As he brought down the curtain on his career in England, the Irish winger was granted a benefit match at Prenton Park on 1 May 1961 against an All-Star XI which included Bryan Douglas, Dennis Stevens, Alan A'Court, Jimmy Armfield, Billy Liddell and Tommy's former Everton teammate

Matt Woods. He was also given a fitting farewell at a civic function hosted by the Mayor of Birkenhead.

Returning to the Emerald Isle, he turned out for (the now defunct) Cork Hibernians. Even at this veteran age, he was selected on multiple occasions for League of Ireland representative sides. Having hung up his boots in 1963, he had no

Tommy the famous butcher, photographed outside his premises in 1991 (credit: Everton FC)

desire to move into football management. He focused on a butcher's business on St Gabriel's Road, Clontarf that had been founded in 1958. As he was still engaged by Tranmere Rovers at that time, Tommy's brother, Kevin, managed the business in his absence. Needless to say, football fans – not just of an Evertonian persuasion – would seek him out at the shop and request autographs or take photographs. In time his son Anthony would take on the most famous butcher's and victualler's in Ireland. Naturally, Tommy met up with Peter Farrell regularly and was saddened by his friend's advancing Alzheimer's. The Farrell and Eglington families have remained close.

A prodigiously talented golfer, he had got the bug from Alex Stevenson in their time together at Everton. 'Stevie' took him to the course in Bootle for instruction (and no doubt some gentle leg-pulling). His first round took 117 strokes and cost him six lost balls, but he soon had his handicap down to single figures and enjoyed a weekly fourball with Peter Farrell, Eddie Wainwright and Don Donovan. While with the Toffees, Tommy twice reached the final of the Professional Footballers' Golf

Championship, coming up against Don Revie, in one of them. In addition to being a member of the Cedars Golfing Society, Tommy was elected captain of the St Anne's club in 1970, at which point he was playing off a handicap of five.

In spite of having no desire to venture in football management after hanging up his boots in 1963, a decade later there was to one foray. When John McSeveney, manager of the resolutely amateur League of Ireland club Home Farm, resigned during the 1973/74 season, Tommy stepped into the breach for the remainder of the season, pending the appointment of Dave Bacuzzi. Twenty years later, the north Dublin club would carry the Everton name in a tie-up with the Merseysiders which only delivered modest benefits for both parties.

Tommy on the golf course, where he excelled (credit: Eglington family)

Tommy's five-goal haul against Doncaster in September 1952, was celebrated a quarter of a century later in somewhat different surroundings, as he recalled to the Everton matchday programme in 1951: 'I was playing golf in Killarney with a group of friends and one of them had noticed it coincided with the anniversary of the Doncaster match. He contacted a newspaper to get the times of my goals and we sat round a table re-living the match. One chap kept an eye on his watch and when it got to the time I had scored, we all cheered and raised our glasses. I can't think what the other people in the bar thought.'

Everton never left Tommy; a copy of the Monday edition of the *Liverpool Echo* was posted to him every week by Terry Egan, the son of his former landlady in

Bootle. He would check the Everton reports first, followed by those of Tranmere and Liverpool ('because I have happy memories of them and their fans too', he explained). He was a regular visitor to Merseyside to take in matches, his children being amazed when young supporters recognised him and asked for autographs. Such trips gave him the opportunity to visit his friend and former Everton teammate Harry Leyland and his wife Margaret – with the hospitality reciprocated in Dublin. He was at Everton's Wembley Cup finals in the mid-1980s and in 1995, the latter in the company of Leyland. He took an interest in the fortunes of Tranmere Rovers, especially under the stewardship of his Goodison and Prenton Park teammate John King, who called in on him when the Wirral outfit was on a break in Ireland. He had planned to attend the League Cup final at Wembley in 1994 but, alas, Rovers were beaten on penalties in the semi-final.

Back home, he watched the Toffees whenever they ventured over the Irish Sea. Tommy was also happy to oblige fans by attending supporters' club functions in Dublin with the Irish Toffees supporters' group and in Cork, where he'd sometimes go with friend and former teammate Don Donovan. Interviewed about his playing career, he once said: 'I think that there was more enjoyment and fun in the days that Peter and I played. There's so much money in the game now, and more pressure on players.'

At the age of 68 Tommy was diagnosed with pancreatic cancer and the prognosis was bleak, but the skills of surgeons gave him a new lease of life. He passed away in 2004, aged 81, having lived with vascular dementia in his final three years. Seven years later a display in his honour was unveiled at the FAI head office in Dublin; during his lifetime he was presented with an FAI merit award at half-time in an international match, as he had come up just short of the 25 caps required to receive an engraved silver shamrock. His children and grandchildren continue to make regular visits to Goodison Park.

We close with remarks Tommy made in 1955, nine years after moving to Merseyside: 'No matter where I might be in the years ahead ... I shall always have a soft spot in my heart for the Goodison Park club and the hundreds of friendly and hospitable folk I have been fortunate to know.'

*Tommy Eglington, a study in concentration as he runs onto the pitch in around 1956.
A terrific servant to Everton, he stands 13th in the all-time club appearance list*

PETER FARRELL'S CAREER STATISTICS

PLAYING CAREER
Appearances by Football League and cup matches

CLUB	APPS	GOALS
Shamrock Rovers (1939–46)		
Everton (1946–57)	422 (13)	34 (4)
Tranmere Rovers (1957–60)	114 (1)	6 (0)
Sligo Rovers (1961)	3	
Holyhead Town (1961–63)		
Drogheda (1963)		
Ireland (FAI)	28	
Ireland (IFA)	7	

MANAGERIAL CAREER
Tranmere Rovers (1957–60)
Holyhead (1961–63)
Drogheda (1963)
T.E.K. United (1964–67 and 1968–71)
St Patrick's Athletic (1967–68)

ACKNOWLEDGEMENTS

This biography would not have been possible without the incredible support of Peter Farrell's amazing family, namely his daughters Betty, Pauline, Sheila and Geraldine. Their generous supply of anecdotes, family information, photographs and cuttings has been a godsend.

My Toffeeopolis collective colleagues Gavin Buckland, Simon Hart and, in particular, James Corbett have been encouraging during the research and writing process.

A number of people have given their time to help turn several iterations of the manuscript into something ready for publication. Francis Hickey has been a superb proofreader, copy-editor and provider of sage advice, while Alison and Peter Jones made a good number of useful observations. Barry Rojack of the Irish Sports Museum provided welcome feedback plus much context to the England against Ireland (FAI) match in 1949, taken from the FAI archives. Finally, Ian Allen gave the manuscript his customary copy-edit to get it in good shape for publication. My thanks go to them all. All errors in the biography are my own.

Fellow members of the wonderful Everton FC Heritage Society have been generous with their support. In addition, I have had help, in varying forms, from Peter Bishop, Pat Brett, John Britton, Brendan Carroll, Brendan Connolly, John Cowell, Gareth M. Davies, Christy Devlin, Pat Devlin, Joe Dodd, Janet Doyle, the Eglington family, David Exall, Gerry Farrell, Jan Grace, Darren Griffiths, Jimmy and

Robert Harris, William Barrington Hill, Dafydd Islwyn, Pat Laverty, Lyndon Lloyd, Mick Meagan, Derville O'Neill, George Orr, Peter Redican, Thomas Regan, Ken Rogers, Mike Royden, Dean Ryan, Billy Smith, Sandy and Gordon Smith, Ray Terry, Toffeeweb readers, Séamus Ua Trodd, Steve Wainwright, the Woods family, Tony Corcoran, John Saunders and the staff at Wirral Library Service.

Unless otherwise stated, images used have been sourced from the Farrell family collection.

My family, Paula, Siân and Ceri, have tolerated me spending countless hours working on this project. I thank them for their forbearance.

Finally, Séamus Coleman very kindly provided the foreword for the book, for which I am extremely grateful.

If I have omitted anyone from the acknowledgements, I apologise.

SELECTED BIBLIOGRAPHY

Books

100 Years of Irish Football – Malcolm Brodie (Blackstaff Press, 1980)

A Football Man – My Autobiography: The Heart of The Game – John Giles (Hodder, 2011)

Everton Greats: Where Are They Now? – Jon Berman and Malcolm Dome (Mainstream Publishing, 1997)

Everton in the 1940s: The Lost Decade – George Orr (self-published via Lulu, 2013)

Everton: The Centenary History – John Roberts (Mayflower, 1980)

Everton: The School of Science – Jame Corbett (Macmillan, 2003)

Faith of Our Families – Edited by James Corbett (deCoubertin, 2018)

Goodison Glory – Ken Rogers (Breedon Books, 2000)

Green is the Colour: The Story of Irish Football – Peter Byrne (Welbeck Publishing, 2012)

Roy Paul: A Red Dragon of Wales – Roy Paul (Robert Hale, 1956)

Soccer in the Boro' – Joe Dodd (Alex Promotions and Publications, 1992)

The Boys in Green: The FAI International Story – Sean Ryan (Mainstream Publishing, 1997)

The Everton Encyclopedia – James Corbett (deCoubertin, 2012)

The Hoops: A History of Shamrock Rovers – Paul Doolan and Robert Goggins (Gill & Macmillan, 1993)

The Official Everton Complete Record – Steve Johnson (deCoubertin, 2016)

Three Sides of the Mersey – Rogan Taylor, Andrew Ward, John Williams (Robson Books, 1993)

Tranmere Rovers: The Complete Record 1884–2009 – Peter Bishop, Steve Wilson, Gil Upton (Breedon Books, 2009)

Tranmere Rovers Football Club – Peter Bishop (Tempus, 1998)

Newspapers, periodicals and match programmes

Birkenhead Advertiser and News

Charles Buchan's Football Monthly

Daily Post (Liverpool and North Wales editions)

Everton FC matchday programmes

Evening Herald

Ireland (FAI) matchday programmes

Irish Times

Irish Independent

Irish Tribune

Liverpool Echo

Liverpool Football Echo

Liverpool Evening Express

Mayo News

North Wales Chronicle

Northern Whig

Sunday Independent

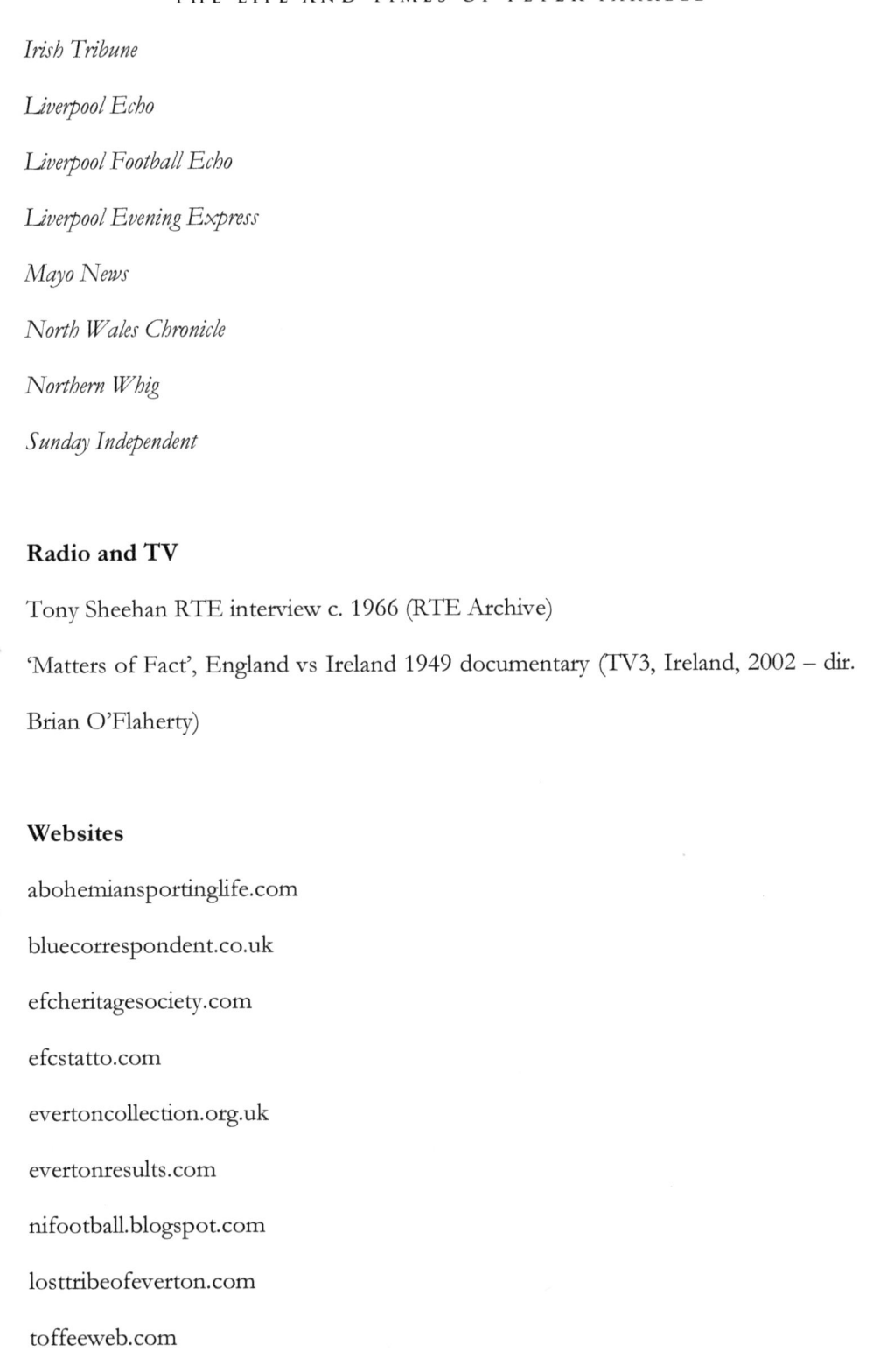

Radio and TV

Tony Sheehan RTE interview c. 1966 (RTE Archive)

'Matters of Fact', England vs Ireland 1949 documentary (TV3, Ireland, 2002 – dir. Brian O'Flaherty)

Websites

abohemiansportinglife.com

bluecorrespondent.co.uk

efcheritagesociety.com

efcstatto.com

evertoncollection.org.uk

evertonresults.com

nifootball.blogspot.com

losttribeofeverton.com

toffeeweb.com

Toffeeopolis

www.mountvernonpublishing.com

www.ingramcontent.com/pod-product-compliance
Ingram Content Group UK Ltd.
Pitfield, Milton Keynes, MK11 3LW, UK
UKHW050741261025
464311UK00010B/16/J